HOW TO DRAW WILD FLOWERS

HOW TO DRAW WILD FLOWERS

by VERE TEMPLE

Author of "Baby Animals on the Farm," etc.

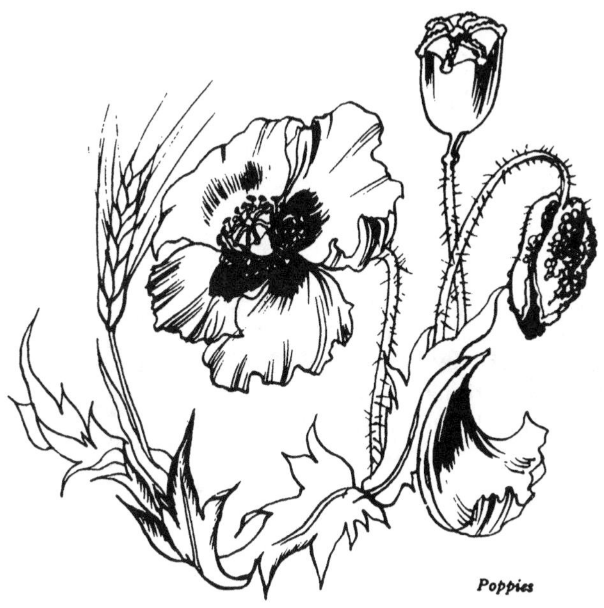

Poppies

COACHWHIP PUBLICATIONS

Greenville, Ohio

To
Jane, John, Joe
and James

How to Draw Wild Flowers, by Vere Temple

First published 1942.

ISBN 1-61646-196-9
ISBN-13 978-1-61646-196-6

CoachwhipBooks.com

CONTENTS

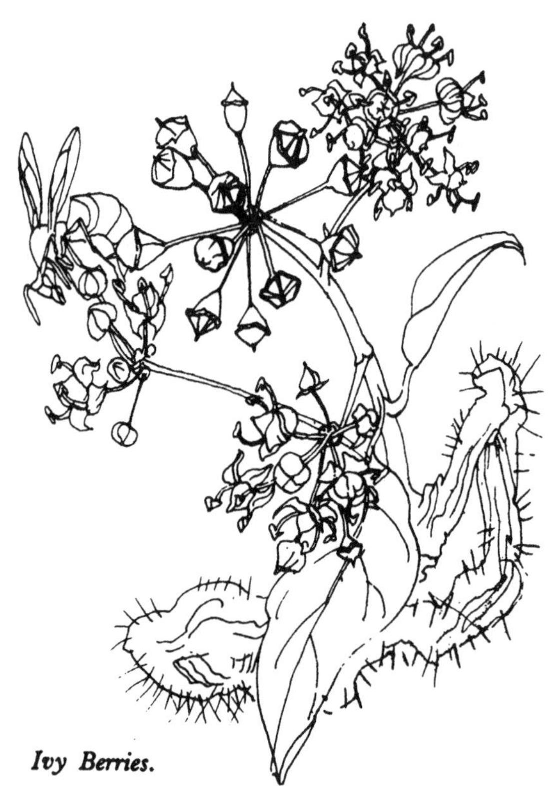

Ivy Berries.

INTRODUCTION

Among the living things round us, the beasts and birds, flowers and butterflies, grasshoppers and snails and curious sea-shells, it is the flowers that appear as our especial friends. The tantalising butterflies fly away as we approach, the birds hide in the thicket, rabbits scuttle into their holes ; but the flowers, the lovely familiar flowers, are ever present to delight us. And to say that they are our friends is not merely a fanciful notion ; for they are useful to us in many ways. We eat their nectar, transformed into honey by the bees ; and the plants give us, also, a variety of remedies for our bodily ills. Country people, since the earliest times, have picked and dried their leaves and made infusions from flowers and roots, for coughs and colds and all manner of ailments. There are books—herbals as they are called—in which you can read about these things, and very interesting they are, and curious, too, for the old cures are bound up with magic and witchcraft and other strange doings.

But I have not space here to tell you about this. It is with the beauty of flowers that I am now concerned, with their shapes and growth and how to draw them. For flowers are such lovely things : nothing in the world seems quite so perfect. They have been an inspiration to artists for hundreds of years.

Long ago the Indians and Persians, in their illuminated books, made wonderful flower-patterns. More famous still are the old Chinese and Japanese brush-drawings and paintings of flowers and plants, executed on scrolls of silk or on rice-paper. Some of these rank among the finest works of art in the world. And in Europe, the Dutch painters depicted flowers with loving care. The Italian masters,

Botticelli and Leonardo and Titian, often introduced plants into their pictures—clumps of columbine or anemones growing out of a rocky landscape, or roses trailing against the sky.

In England, and also in Ireland, France and Germany, the mediaeval monks studied flowers minutely, weaving them into rich borders for their illuminated Missals. They put birds among the flowers, and butterflies and animals, and painted them with brilliant colours and with gold. Then, when printing was invented, a great tradition of book-illustrations grew out of this manuscript painting, and the herbals were made, with careful engravings of

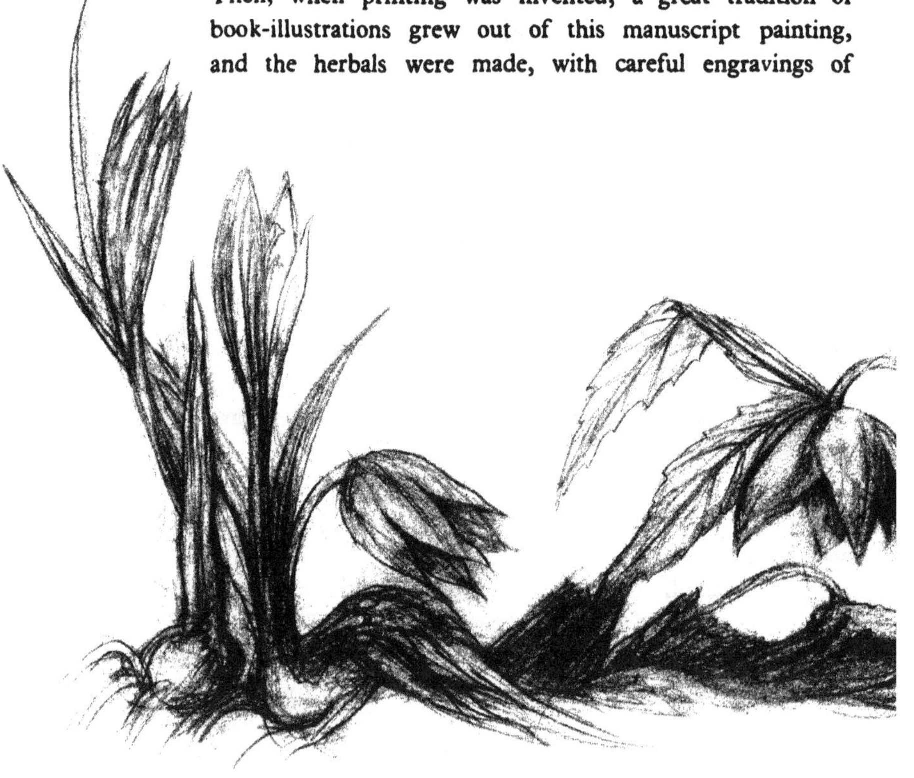

plants rather formally arranged ; they are most interesting as records of flowers that grew in gardens in bygone days, and excellent too as designs, from the artist's point of view.

About a hundred and forty years ago, more flower-books were made—printed in colour by a process called lithography. These are most life-like portraits of flowers, and a great many of them are very beautiful.

So, you see, people all over the world have always loved painting flowers. And why shouldn't you ? It is given to few of us to be masters, but I think that many of you will be

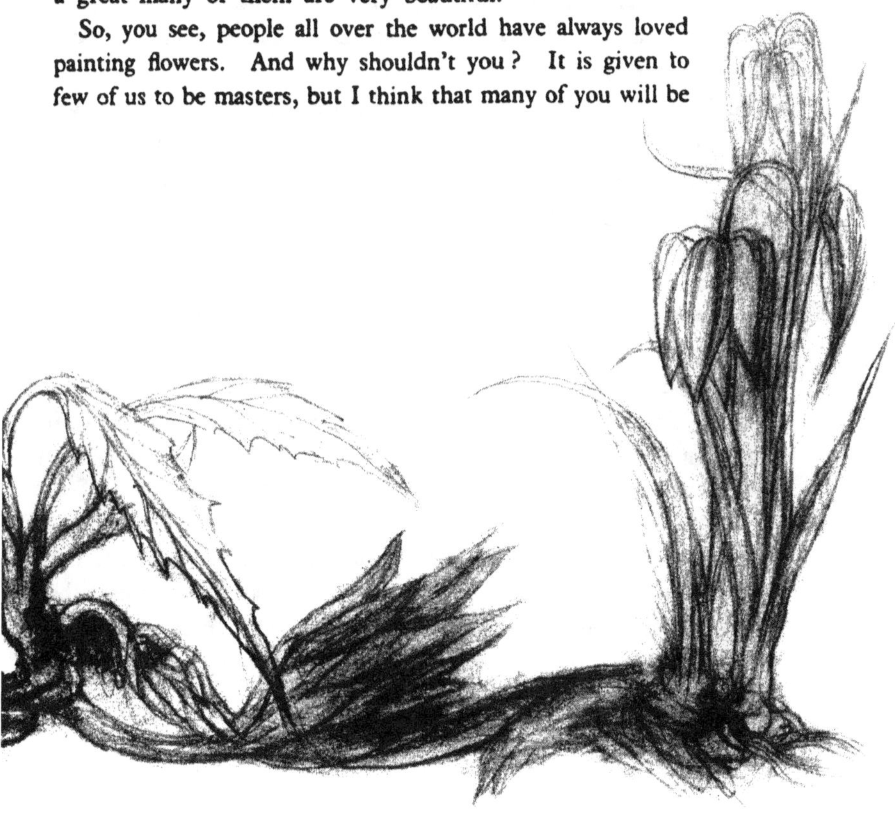

able to draw flowers well, even beautifully, *if* you are really interested in them. It all depends on that *if*. Passionate interest is essential to the production of good drawings. You must study the life and growth of plants as well as the shapes and colours of leaves and blossoms ; this will help you to draw them with love and understanding. If you have a garden, and can grow them from seeds and cuttings, so much the better ; you will then become familiar with them in their different stages. And so, out of enthusiasm, knowledge will grow ; for the humblest weed is a treasure-house of interest if looked at with a seeing eye.

And when you draw and paint the plants that you love, do it your own way—the way that you feel to be right. Use any medium you like—chalk, watercolour, pencil—take a stub of charcoal, an old nail, anything, as long as you enjoy using it.

Here there are short cuts to knowledge, and I hope to be able to help you. For instance, one difficulty that arises when drawing flowers is the small size of many of the forms of flowers and their details, such as stamens and pistil. I have therefore given you " close-up " enlargements of some of the flower-heads. The flowers I have drawn are all common wild ones, easily found on any country walk. I have chosen wild flowers because they interest me particularly, both by reason of their grace and of the difficulties with which they have to contend. Garden flowers, pampered in prepared plots, weeded and tended and watered, have an easy time ; but the wild plants have to struggle along as best they may—over-crowded, parched by summer drought, their seeds blown hither and thither on to poor soil ; fragile, yet hardy creatures, arising each Spring to charm us anew.

In the next chapter I will tell you something of these wild things and of their life and growth. Then we will begin to draw them.

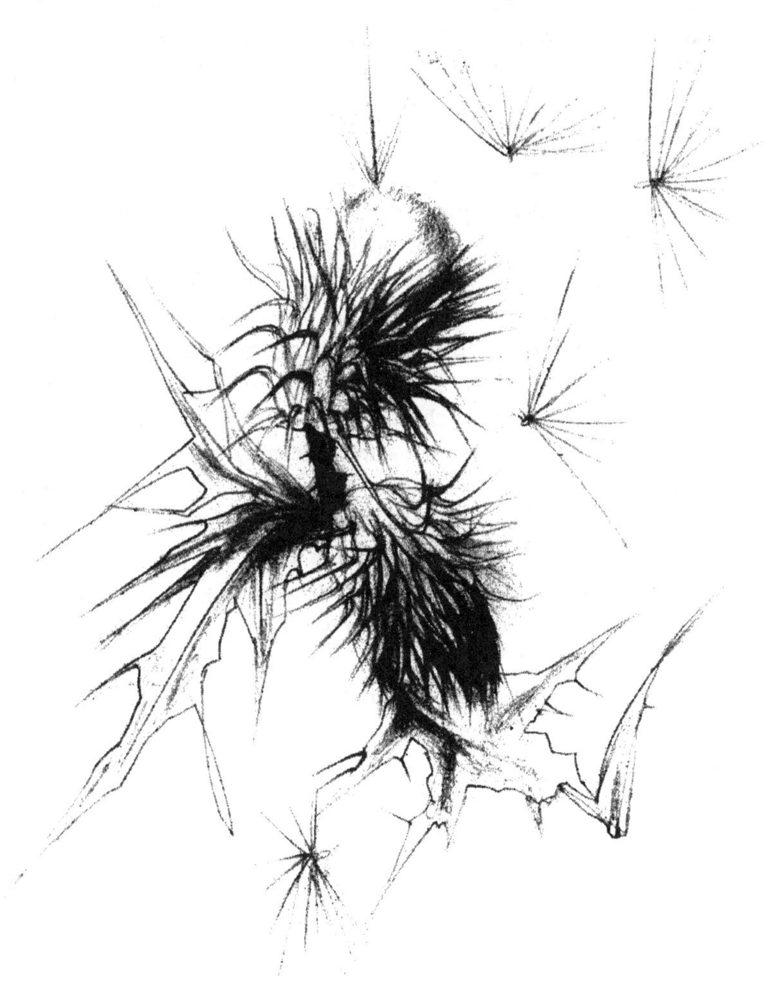

HOW PLANTS EAT,

Flowers cannot move about, and have to live rooted to one place ; but they are nevertheless very much alive. They breathe and grow and eat and produce children like other living creatures, but in a different way from the beasts and birds and butterflies and fishes. Animals eat with their mouths : plants eat and drink with their leaves and with their roots. All those root-fibres, that you see when you pull up a plant, are busy extracting nourishment from the soil ; but they must have it in liquid form. That is why we have to water our garden flowers, and why all plants grow after a shower. The rain seeps through the soil, and the roots are then able to extract from the wet earth the lime, or the iron, or other mineral substances, upon which they thrive. And just as some animals eat meat, others grass, and others fruit, so some plants like one sort of food, some another. Violets and cowslips like chalk and lime ; but foxgloves avoid it, and you will never find them growing on chalky soil. Roots have other functions too. They hold down plants that might well be top-heavy and fall over were they not firmly anchored. And many plants increase by means of their roots, which creep along the ground, sending up new plants at intervals. White clover, violets, and restharrow are instances of this and there are many others that you will be able to find out for yourself. So you see that roots are all-important to the flower, and to draw a plant without them is like making a portrait of a person without a mouth.

Roots grow into all kinds of queer and interesting shapes, which you can observe for yourselves by pulling up hedgerow plants or garden weeds.

On pages 8 and 9 I have drawn some of these shapes in a design of spring flowers which was suggested by watching the movements of flames in a fire.

Now, (you will say) how in the world can plants *breathe*? Well, they breathe with their leaves. The surface of every green leaf is pitted with holes, or pores, so tiny that you can only see them with a high-powered microscope; and through these holes the plant breathes in gases from the atmosphere and gives out others. During the day-time, under the influence of light, the leaf absorbs a gas called carbon dioxide and gives out another called oxygen: and at dusk it breathes out carbon dioxide. With the help of the sunshine, the plant transforms this carbon into food for itself—sugar and starch, which it stores up in its body. The sunlight helps it to make, also, the green colour for its leaves. I expect you have often seen *white* leaves growing inside the chink of a door or under a heap of rubbish; these are white because they have not been exposed to the light and so the plant has not been able to make any green colour to tint them. And not only is the leaf a kind of extra mouth for the plant: it helps to keep it at the right temperature—neither too hot nor too cold, by giving off surplus water in the form of vapour, through the tiny pores that I have mentioned. So you see that the plant is not only alive, but busy; it is a kind of little factory, making all sorts of good things to eat, and very sensibly, storing some of the food up for next year. You have probably noticed the yellow flowers of the coltsfoot, that blossom in

February before the leaves appear. Well, they are produced from food stored up by the plant from the summer before.

But before it can do all this, the plant has to grow up from a seed, shed from the parent plant in the late summer or autumn. Sometimes the seeds lie in the earth all winter before they germinate (as it is called) and grow into plants ; sometimes they develop into plants at once and pass the winter as seedlings. The seeds are able to grow because, in the centre of each, and protected by the outer husk, there is a spark of life called the germ. This is imbedded in a wrapping of food good for baby plants. These nourish the tiny sprouting thing until it has strength to throw out roots of its own. On page 15 you will see a drawing of some turnip seeds germinating. These, of course, are not wild plants ; I chose them because they grow easily and I could plant them in a pot and watch them. See how the baby plant creeps out of the seed, while the husk drops off and rots. One plant is still wearing the husk on the tip of its root. Up, up they come, little white coils—white because there is no light underground to colour them green. And just as babies are born with downy hair, that falls out and is replaced by new locks as they grow bigger, and as puppies and kittens shed their first fluffy coats and grow thicker, stronger fur, so the baby plant starts life with a pair of leaves quite unlike those of the grown-up plant. Some kinds of plant have two of these seed-leaves, some one only. Turnips have two. On the right side of the drawings is a turnip, older than the others, with grown-up leaves and quite a nice root. You could grow mustard and cress on wet flannel and watch all this happening for yourself.

Seeds can be all sorts of shapes—round—ribbed—pointed. And the parent plant has various devices for getting them into new places, so that the young plants shall have a good start in life. Thistles, as you know, have seeds fastened to rosettes of down that are blown hither and thither by the wind. There is no prettier sight than these gossamer puffs sailing along against the blue sky on an autumn morning. Dandelions have clocks, each seed of which is shaped like a little parachute borne in the

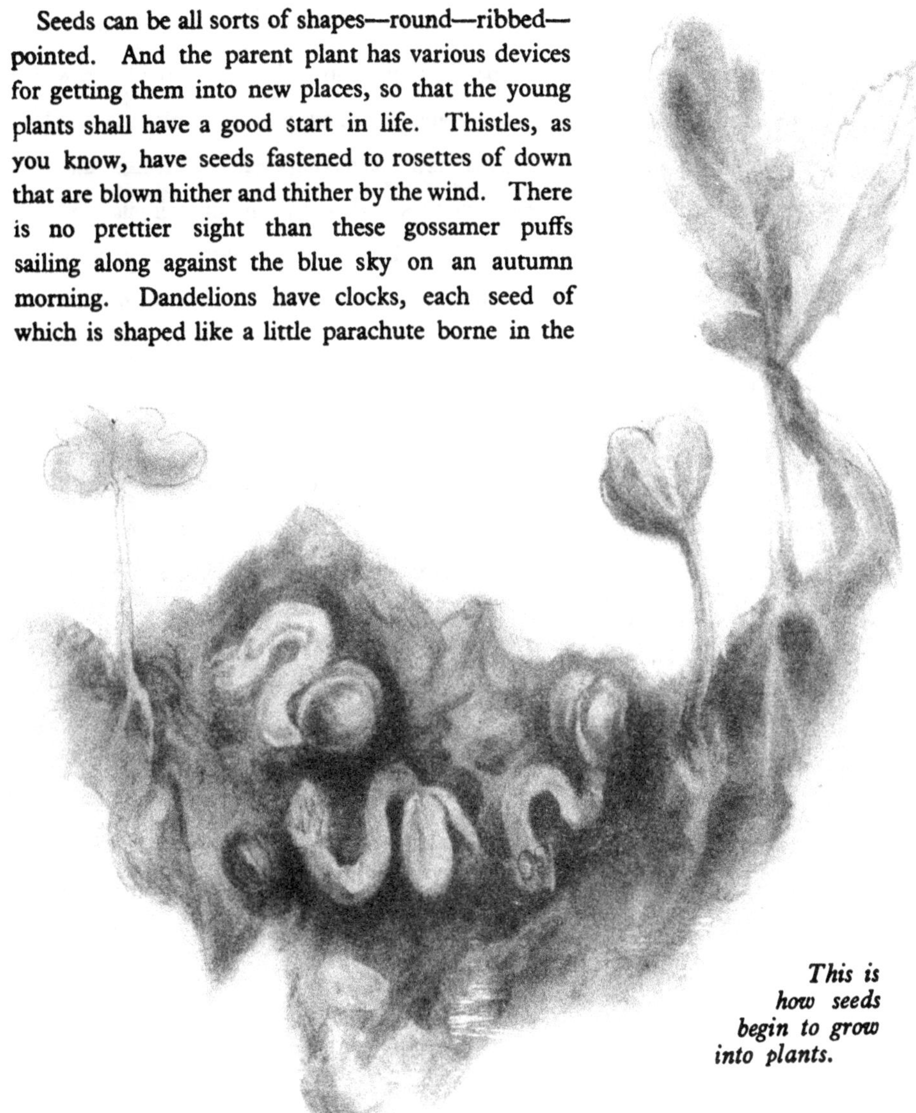

This is how seeds begin to grow into plants.

same way by the wind. When the parachute shuts, the seed drops to earth and takes root, and by and by a new dandelion plant comes up. Burdocks and Goosegrass have seeds encased in sheaths that become entangled in people's clothes and in the fur of animals, and are eventually rubbed off somewhere a considerable distance away, so that these plants, too, start life in a new place. (See drawings on pages 18 and 19).

The Balsam has a seedpod that, when ripe, explodes like a small pistol, shooting out the seeds (see drawing page 17). And the seed of the wood-spurge, when warmed by the sun, hops from its sheath into a plot of new ground. All these things are fascinating to observe, and they make good drawings—roots and seeds and pods are, I think, just as interesting as the blossoms themselves and they are good subjects for you to start on, because there is not much colour to distract your attention from the forms—those queer, lacy shapes, and dagger-shapes, and circles and ovals and oblongs, that you can copy, simply at first, with a sharp pencil or pen and ink. But as these shapes are small it will help you to draw them through a low-powered lens or a watchmaker's glass that fits under your eyebrow leaving your hands free. Through this magnifying glass you will perceive the perfection of finish of the seeds and of the buds and other details of the plant.

Pay great attention to the stalks for they are the supply lines for the food that passes from the root to leaves, and from leaves to tubers and growing parts.

Notice too, that some leaves grow opposite each other, others alternately, some in whorls (as a circle is called) and that some spread up from the root like flames shooting upwards. And if you want to make a detailed drawing, pull up the plant and draw it complete with its root,

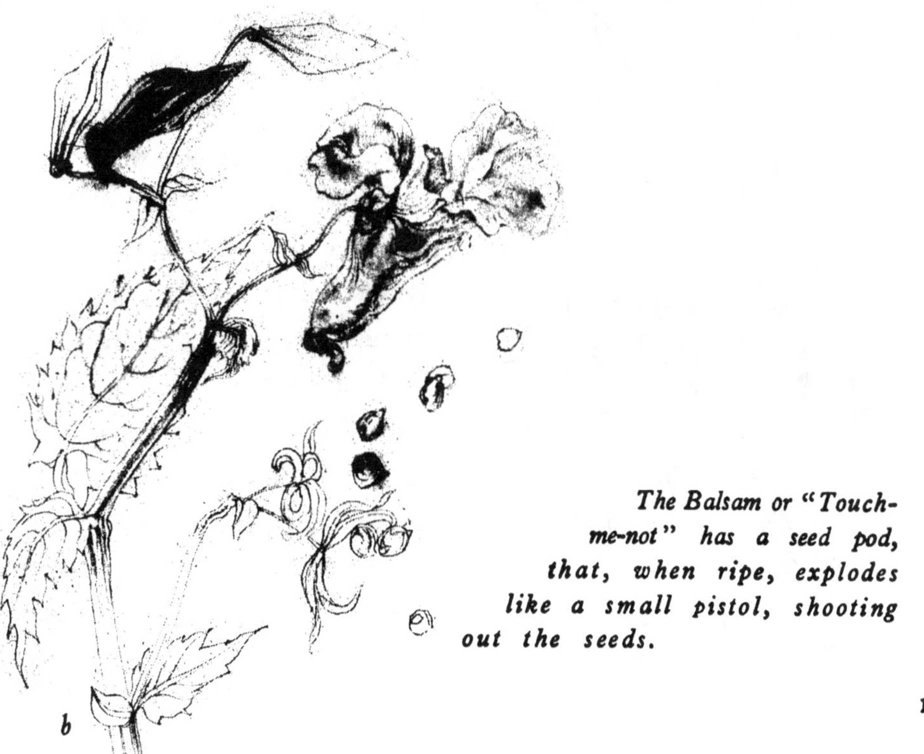

The Balsam or "Touch-me-not" has a seed pod, that, when ripe, explodes like a small pistol, shooting out the seeds.

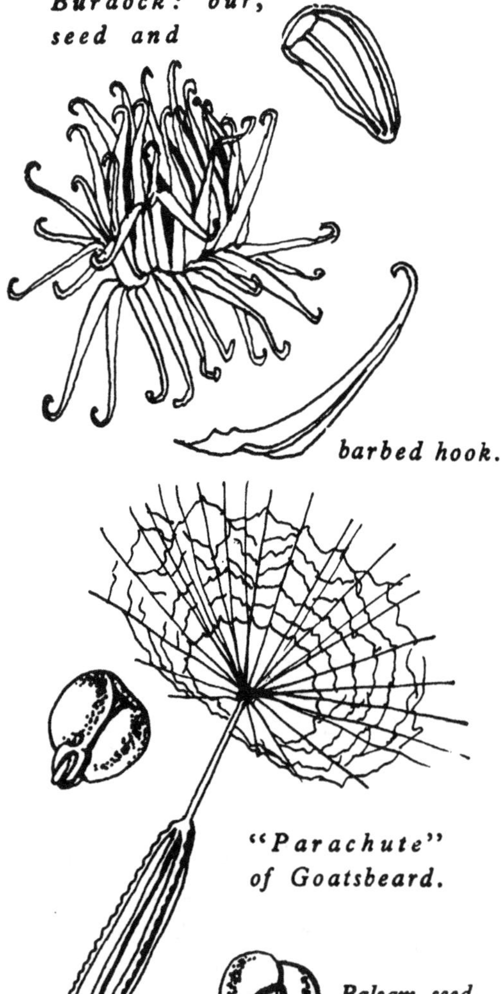

Burdock: bur, seed and barbed hook.

"Parachute" of Goatsbeard.

Balsam seed.

HOW PLANTS EAT, which you can arrange spread out nicely in a pleasing pattern beneath its stems and leaves.

For painting the flowers, you will need three camel-hair brushes, a fat one, a middle-sized one and a thin one with a good point; a white saucer also, on which to spread your dabs of water-colour paint. This should be bought in tubes, which are easier to handle and to keep clean than cakes of colour. Cobalt is the nicest blue, deep cadmium and aureolin the brightest yellows; two sorts of green can be made by mixing each yellow with the blue, and a different green by adding a little lamp-black. With rose

"Seeds can be all

madder used alone, you can paint pink flowers, and purple ones by mixing it with cobalt. For poppies and other red flowers, vermilion is best; a queer exciting colour comes by adding black to it. Sepia is a useful brown. Chinese white added to any of these colours thickens and alters them; but if you are a beginner it is best to use the colours as cleanly as possible and to make your experiments by degrees.

But I am not going to tell you much about drawing until the chapter after next, for we must now return to our young plants and see how they are growing up in their new surroundings.

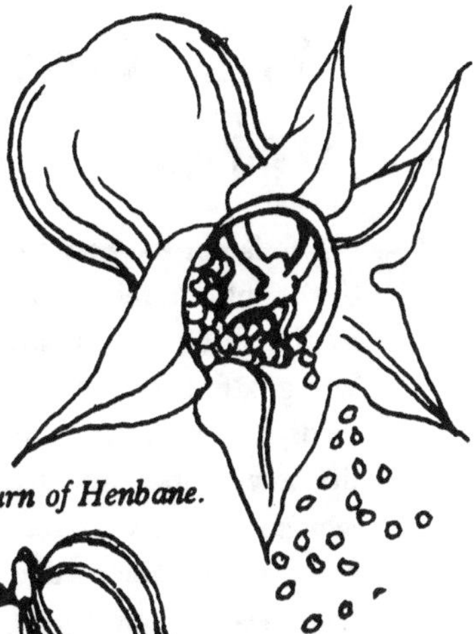

Seed urn of Henbane.

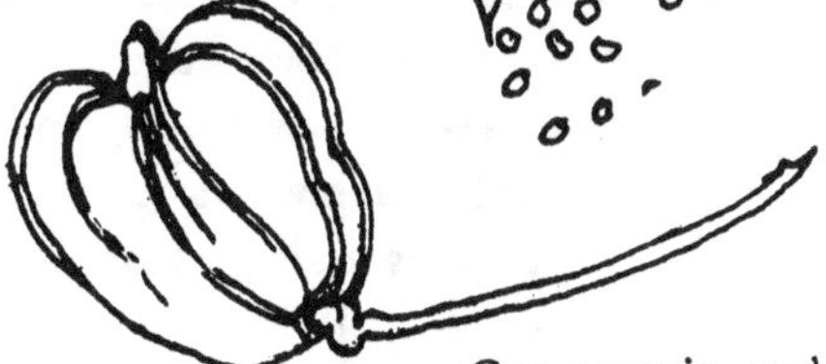

Cow-parsnip seed

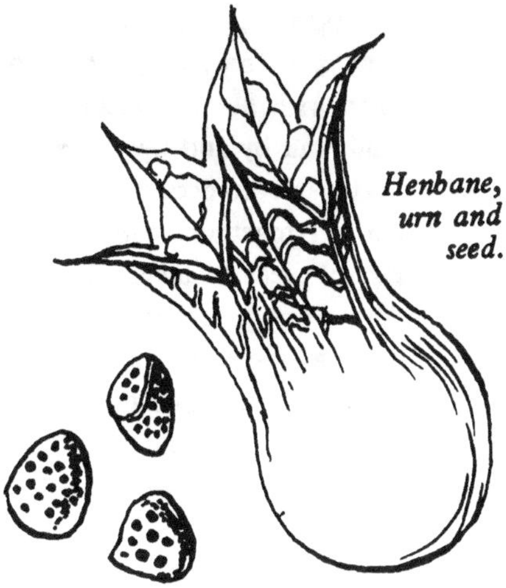

Henbane, urn and seed.

sorts of shapes."

THE GROWN-UP PLANT AND ITS FLOWERS

Life is not too easy for them at first. Lots of the seeds are washed by the autumn rains into places where no plant can grow—tarry patches by the side of the road, and among stones where there is no earth. The goldfinches come in twittering flocks and eat many of the thistle-seeds, and the farmer cuts down the rest; and the cottagers weed up the sow-thistles and dandelions and groundsel from their gardens, which is just as well, for all these plants are pests. But other seedlings come up in the hedgerows and woods—lovely things, primroses, nettle-leaved companula, and pink mallow, and by the river, bur-marigold that nods its head like a miniature sunflower. And, goodness, what a crowd all pushing up at once! For all mixed up with these are dead-nettle and vetches and poppies and stitchwort and dozens more, that all have to take their turn in the sun before they disappear underground to make room for others in the cycle of the year's growth. And then the slugs, eat a good many and a hungry cow munches some with her mouthfuls of grass. However, the sun and rain are kind, and by and by we see the flowers in bud, and then in blossom.

Has it ever occurred to you that all the gaily-coloured flowers are not put together anyhow but that each one is a most beautiful and careful piece of mechanism? Pick a flower to bits and you will see that every part has its use.

First—those green scales wrapping up the bud—they are called sepals, and protect the young flower as it is forming. When the

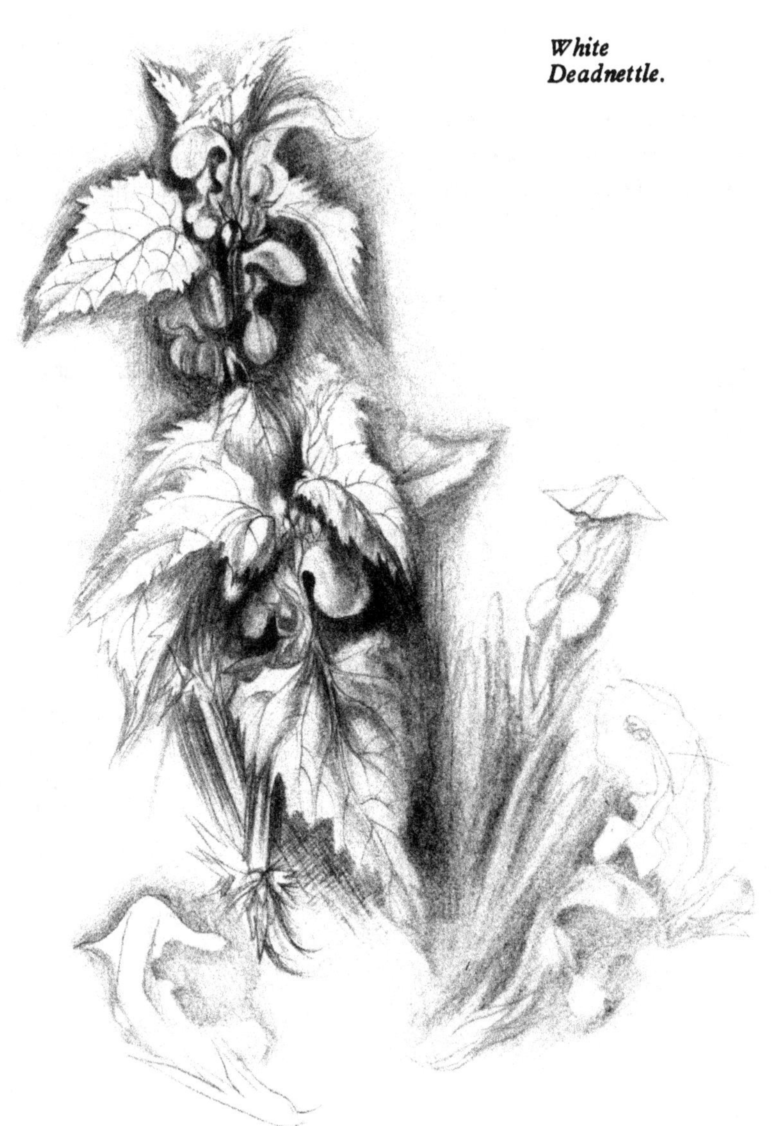

White Deadnettle.

flower opens, the sepals curl back, and we see the petals. Sometimes these are separate, as in the rose ; sometimes they are joined, rather in the form of an umbrella, as in the convolvulus. and sometimes they form a tube, as in the snapdragon. Their brilliant colours are a signal to the bees and butterflies that nectar is here, and pollen, and will the guests please come to the feast? And when the insects arrive, attracted also by the scent of the flower, the cunning plant sees to it that some of the yellow pollen from the centre of the flower is rubbed on to their wings and legs and furry bodies. Thus it is carried to other flowers, where it

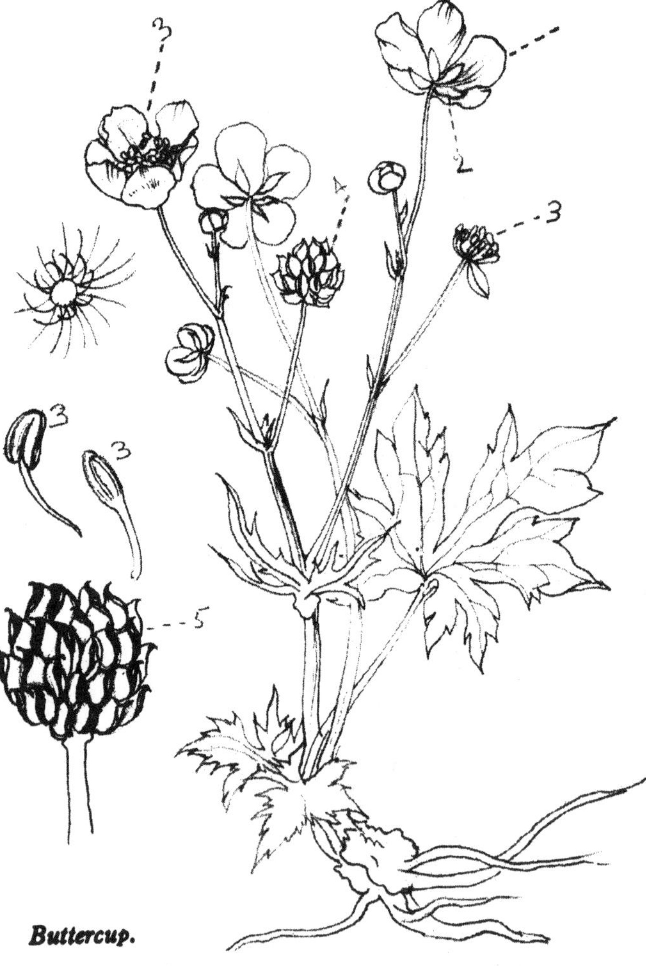

Buttercup.

comes into contact with the seed producing parts, the pistils, which are tubes opening into little caskets called ovaries. When it receives this golden pollen, the ovary swells and alters in shape and by and by, when the flower withers, it turns into the seed,—which would never have ripened at all had it not been touched with golden dust by the butterflies and the industrious bees. The pistil and ovary therefore have the place of honour, in the centre of each flower, with the stamens round them.

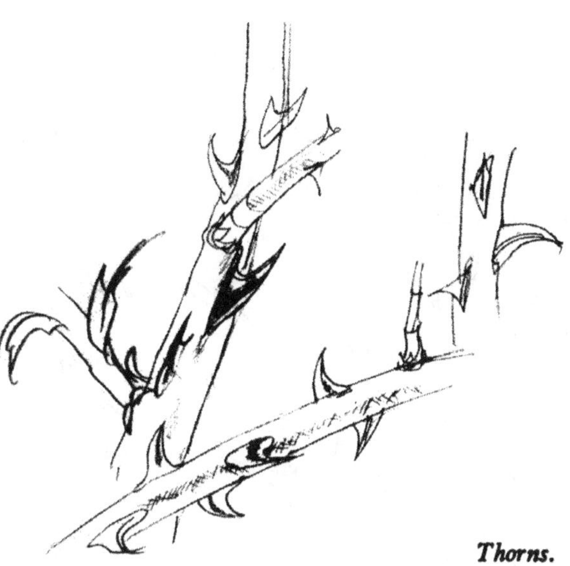

Thorns.

On page 22 is a simple drawing of a buttercup showing the different parts : (1) petal, (2) sepals, (3) stamens, (4) ovary, (5) seeds ripening. This is a dull drawing, little more than a map of the flower. It may, however, help you to start drawing flowers in this way, because you can thus see the proportions of leaf and flower and the length of stem and so on. But it is not a good plan to go on drawing in this map-like manner. It is better to use a free brush-stroke, as in the studies on pages 34 and 35. Or you can use pencil as in the drawings on pages 28 and 29. Keep a sketch-book always at hand and make drawings of the plants growing, and of interesting details. There is no better way of learning.

RHYTHM AND

SPRING

And now we come to an important subject : that of Rhythm and Movement in drawing. I want you to become interested in this now, at the beginning of your studies, because the qualities of Rhythm and Movement are essential to good work. Without them, your drawings will be dull and lifeless, not worth doing.

Rhythm is the quality of flow-

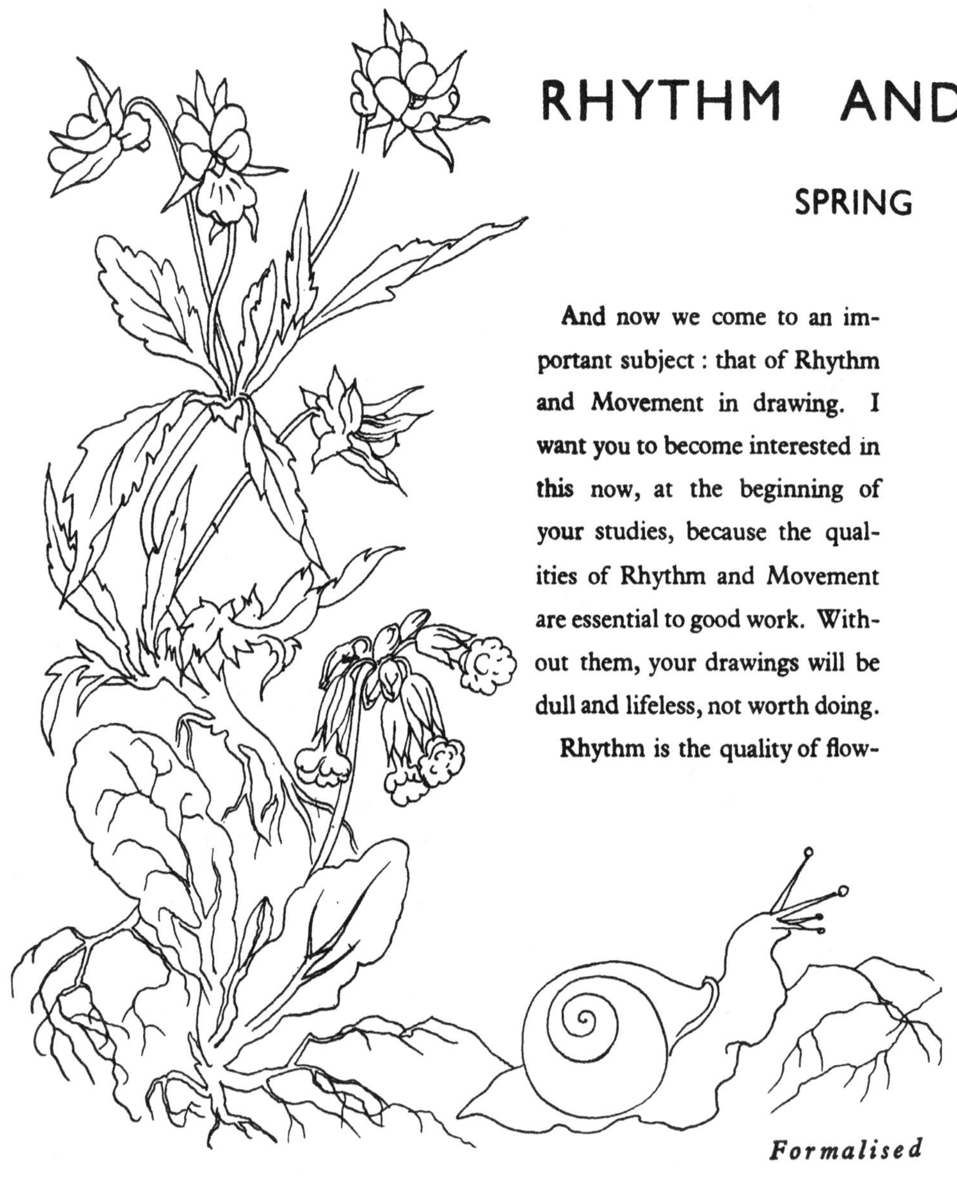

Formalised

MOVEMENT

FLOWERS

ing line, of lovely curves and shapes that answer each other as the echo the sound. You have only to look around you to see that Nature is full of rhythm. The shapes of the clouds, hurrying across the sky, make one kind of Rhythm (see page 26) the growing grass-blades another (see page 27—top), while the daisy on page 28 has a circular rhythm.

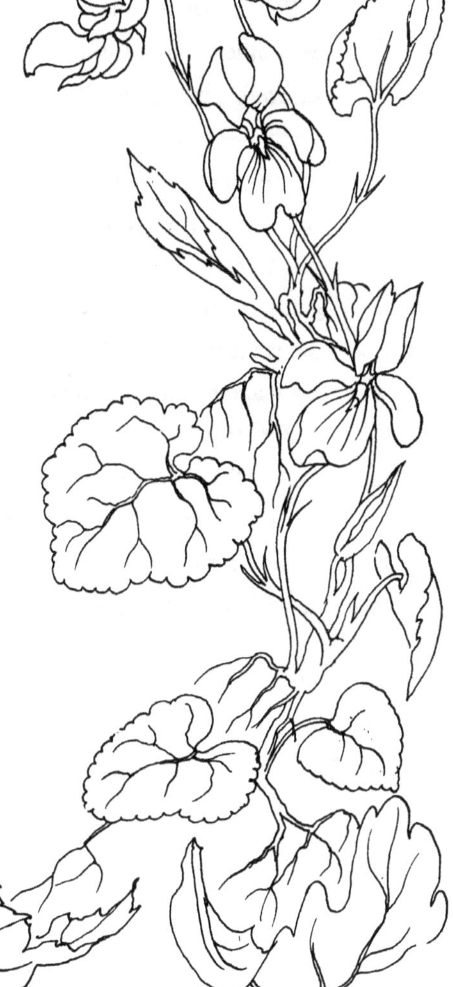

design with Pansies, Cowslips and Violets.

RHYTHM AND MOVEMENT: SPRING FLOWERS

You see what I mean? The leaves and main lines of growth repeat each other in a pattern, which you must accentuate in your drawing. Before beginning to draw a plant, look at it carefully to observe its rhythm—in other words, to see its characteristic lines of growth. These you must seize upon and put down on the paper, leaving out any lines that seem to confuse or spoil the main curves. It will help you to make scribbled diagrams of these main lines first of all, as a guide to the finished drawing. This you can begin when you have the rhythm of the plant clear in your mind. As an example of this, see my diagrams of a convolvulus on page 47, and the accompanying text.

Rhythm is a quality that belongs to all life—the flight of birds, the dance, the growth of flowers. *Movement* means much the same-thing—with this difference: there can be movement without rhythm, as in the awkward movements of an ungainly animal, but there can be no rhythm without the movement of flowing lines and lovely curves.

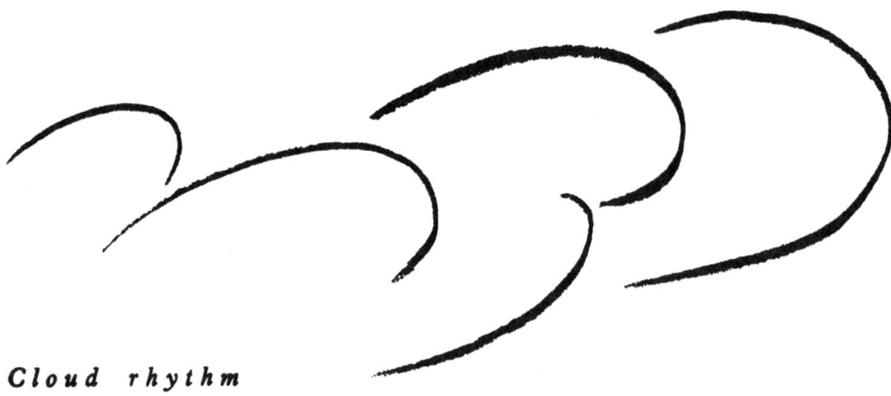

Cloud rhythm

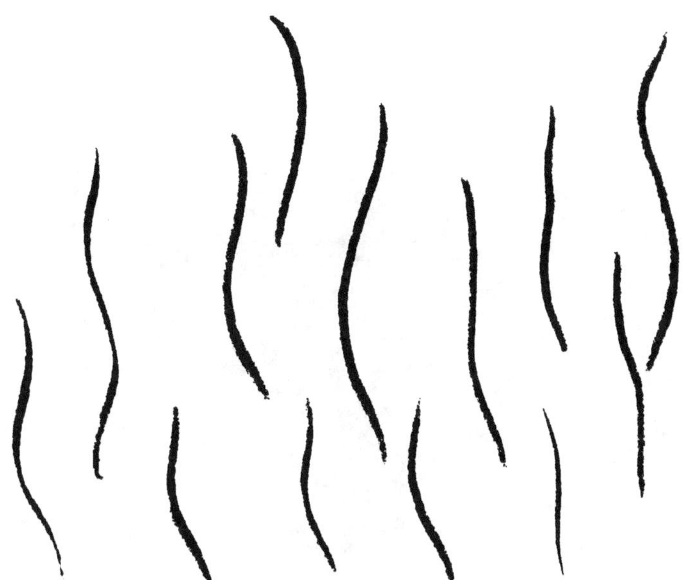

Grass blades.

To say that a drawing has movement does not, of course, mean that it moves from place to place. It means that the artist has been able to express the essential rhythm of the subject he has chosen—

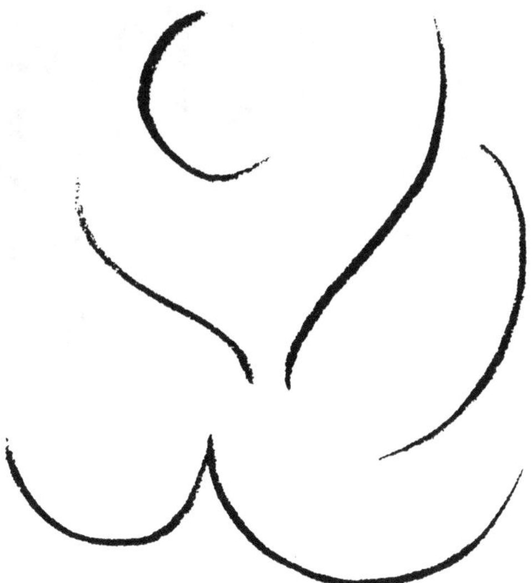

Circular Daisy rhythm.

Daisies.

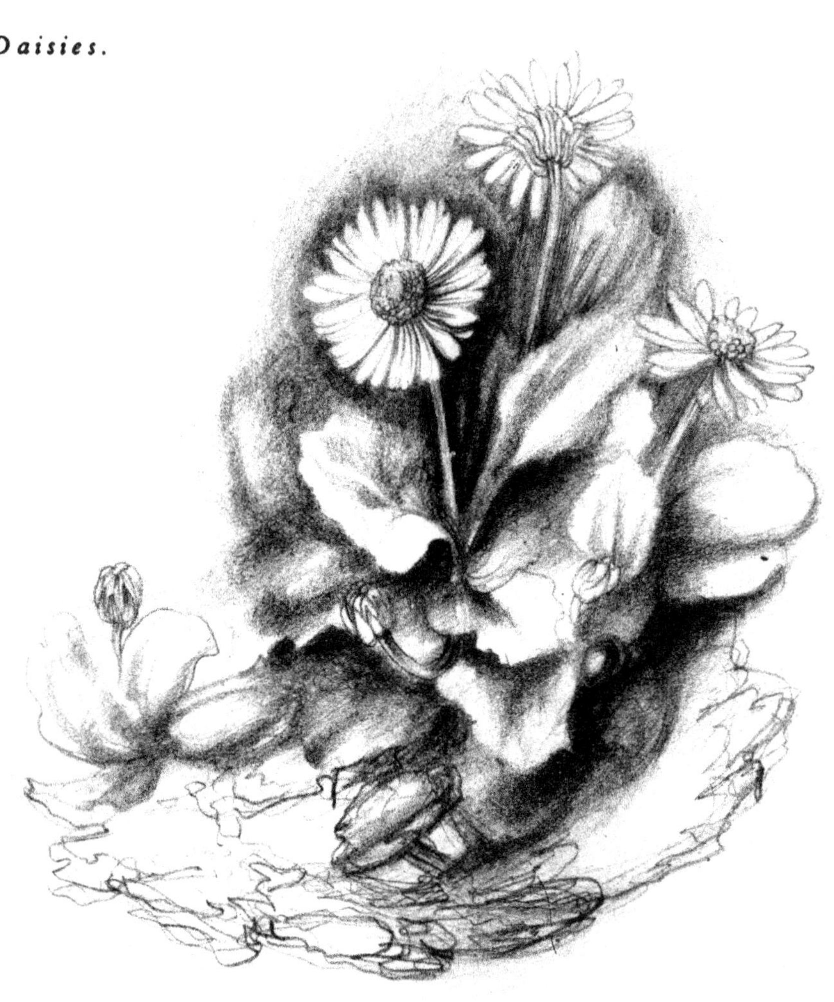

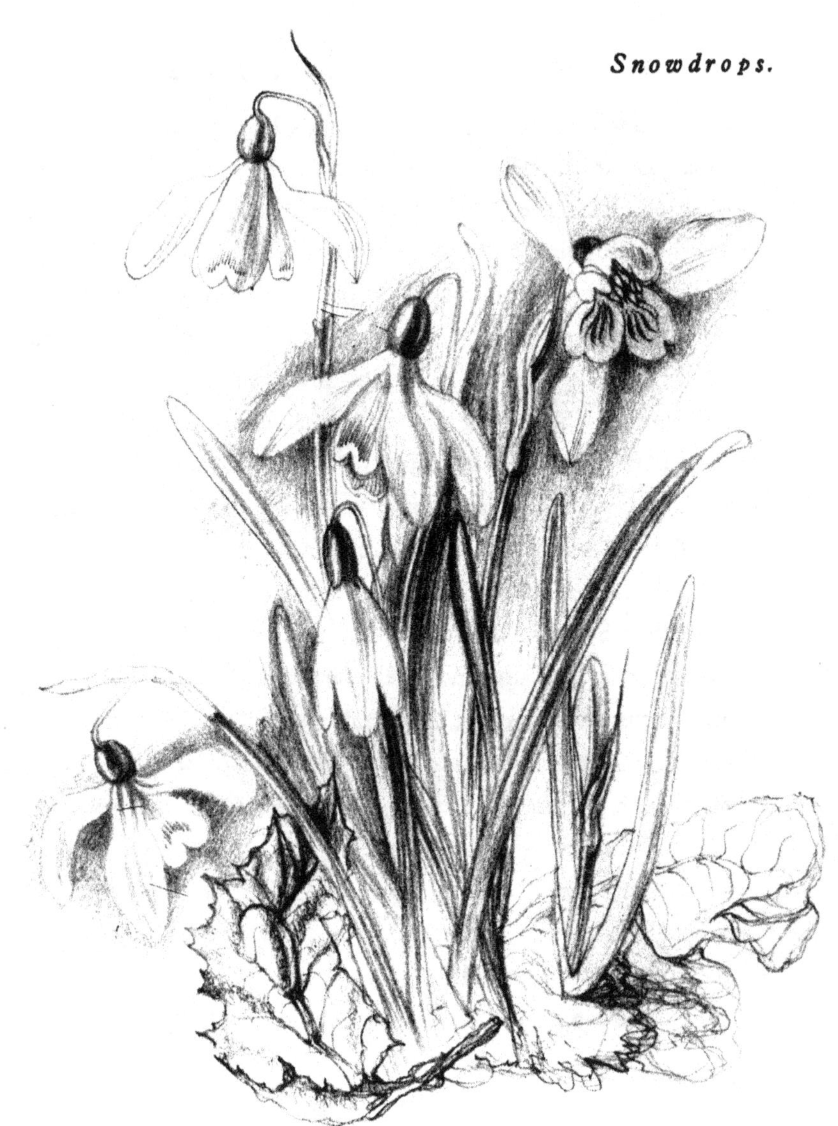

Snowdrops.

be it animals, landscape, groups of people, or plants with their pattern of stems, blossoms and leaves.

When observing the latter you will notice that there are normally two rhythms going on at the same time. The stalks, pointing to the sky, make an upright design; the leaves, spreading out to the sun, appear as frills, or fans, round them. Opposite rhythms can likewise be seen by looking at the reeds, that rise out of the river between the floating saucers of the water lily leaves. If you make a tracing on tissue paper of the cloud rhythm on page 26 and lay it over the diagram of grass-blades opposite, you will see how the two sets of lines can be combined. With a little ingenuity these main lines can be transformed into stems and leaves each with its natural shape, to which you can add the lovely pattern of the veining.

Lines going upwards and lines going across are the first to look for. Corkscrew lines are important too, and are everywhere to be seen in the twining stems and tendrils of plants—hop, bryony, convolvulus, cucumber; but they are more difficult to draw.

Spring flowers have the simplest lines. In summer, when the ground is a maze of flowers, your eye wanders among a complicated pattern of growth. Here you must sort out for yourself the characteristics of each plant.

Let us now turn the page and look at some of them.

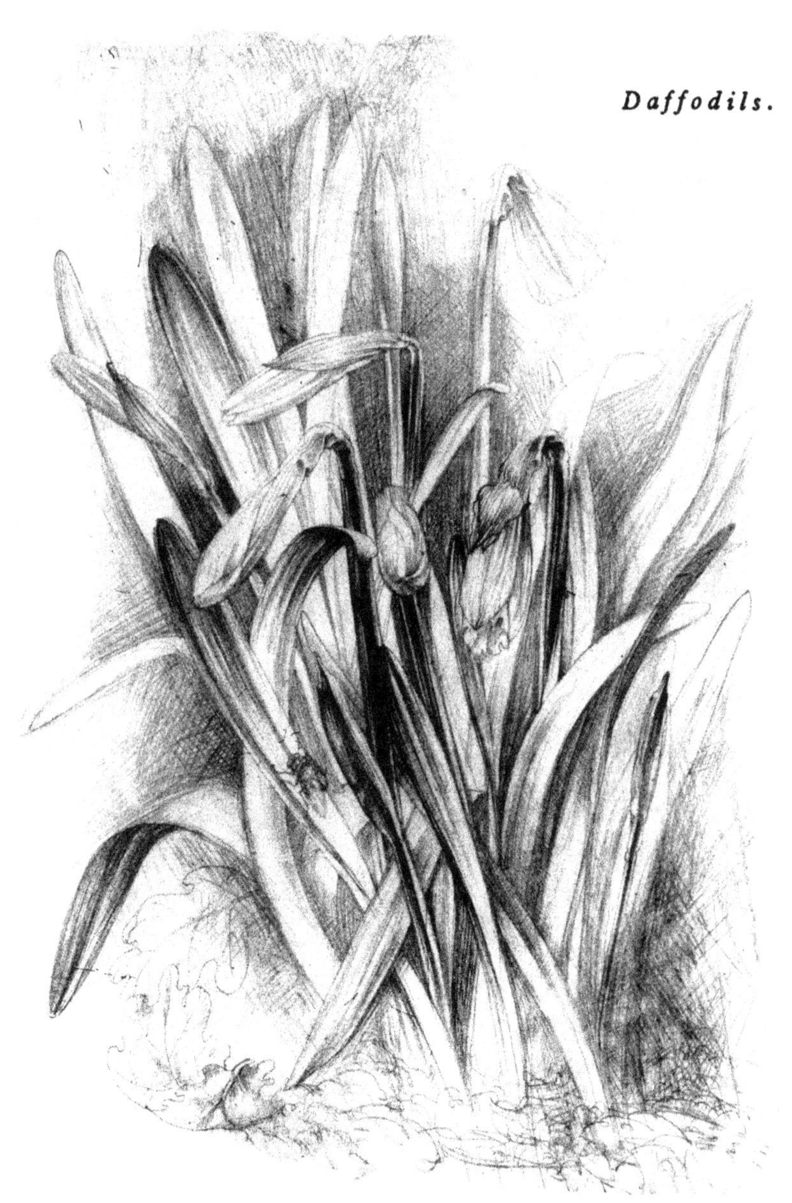

Daffodils.

SUMMER FLOWERS

As you wander among the fields and woods, picking flowers and observing their different ways of growth, you see that they are not *flat* shapes, but that each flower-head, or bud, or stem, is a solid object. Buds are like cups, or urns : stems are like tubes, or cylinders. This *form* of plants is another important thing. You must show it in your drawings, or they will look flat, like shapes cut out of paper.

It is not difficult to learn how to draw form. There are certain common-sense rules that apply to most shapes, and you can use your intelligence in following them. For instance, you want to draw the fat, round seedpods of the yellow water-lily—" brandy-bottles " as the children call them, but you can't make your drawing look solid. Well, take a " brandy-bottle " and place it on the table in front of you so that the light from the window falls on one side. You will see that

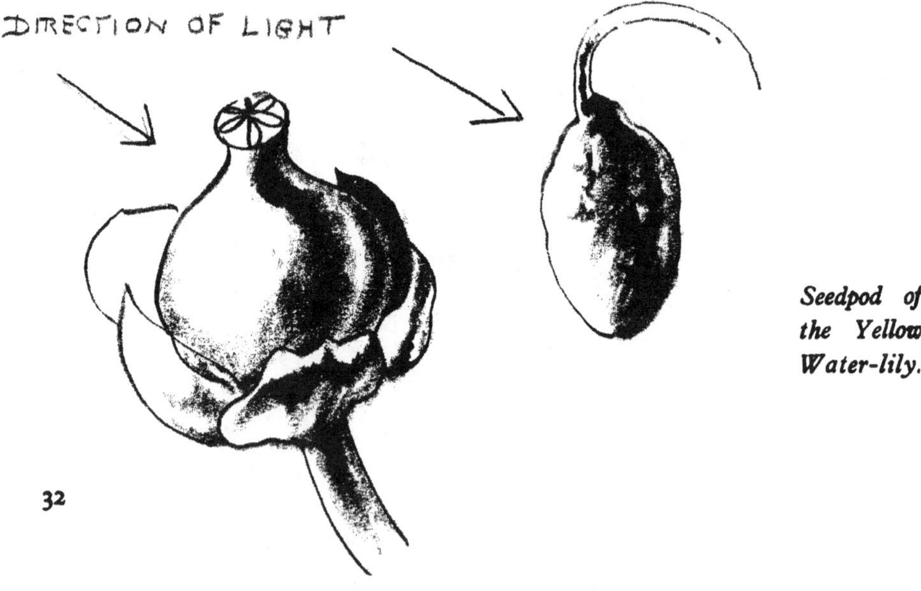

Seedpod of the Yellow Water-lily.

the light shines brightly on that side of the globe-like surface. As the form curves away from the light into shadow, it becomes dark. On the side furthest from the window, light reflected from the bright side illumines it again, but more dimly than on the side next the window. You can observe this in a ball, or an egg, or any other round object. If you draw these patches of light and shade correctly, your " brandy-bottle " will at once appear round. The same rule applies to the stalk, which is a rounded cylinder, or to the egg-shaped bud of the poppy, or to any other solid object.

Water-lilies belong to the streams and ponds, and so I have drawn them with a movement like water-bubbles blown upwards. (Pages 34 and 35). For this study I used a brush and lamp-black water-colour mixed with a little Chinese white, floated on to damp japanese rice-paper. And here is another drawing (page 36) a pencil sketch of the water-lily growing in the stream among its big flat leaves. Here and there are the spear-shaped leaves of the arrow-head, that in late summer throws up three-petalled flowers on a straight stem.

In the water-lily, the stamens are arranged in a circle round the centre of the flower. But they make different patterns in different kinds of flowers. Sometimes they are hidden inside the petals, as in these two plants of the same family, restharrow and clover (pages 37, 38 and 39). These have petals that curve together in the form of a boat, with sails above and a keel below ; and inside the boat, out of sight, are the stamens and seed-producing parts. In the restharrow, as you see, the flowers grow singly on the stem, while in the clover a cluster of them make the sweet-scented head that must be familiar to all of you. The restharrow, like the water lilies, is drawn with a brush.

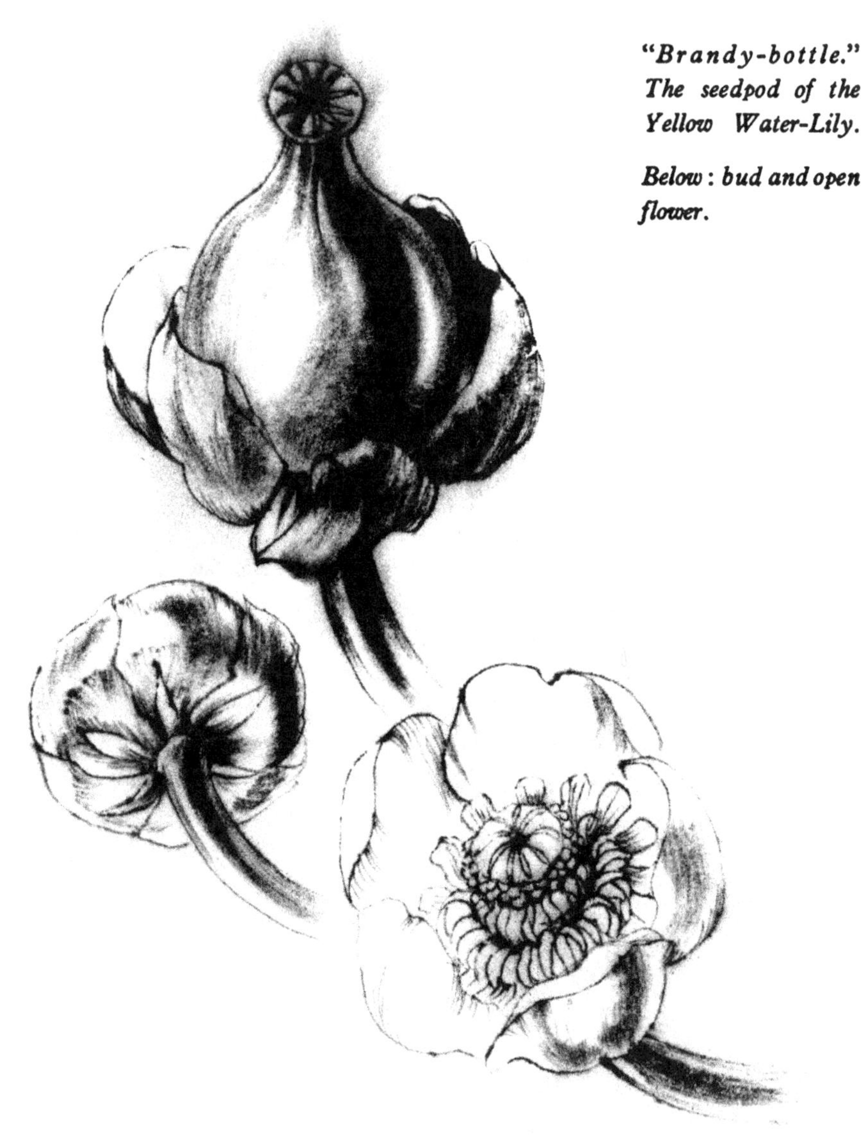

"Brandy-bottle." The seedpod of the Yellow Water-Lily.

Below: bud and open flower.

Studies of the pattern made by the seed-producing parts of the flower.

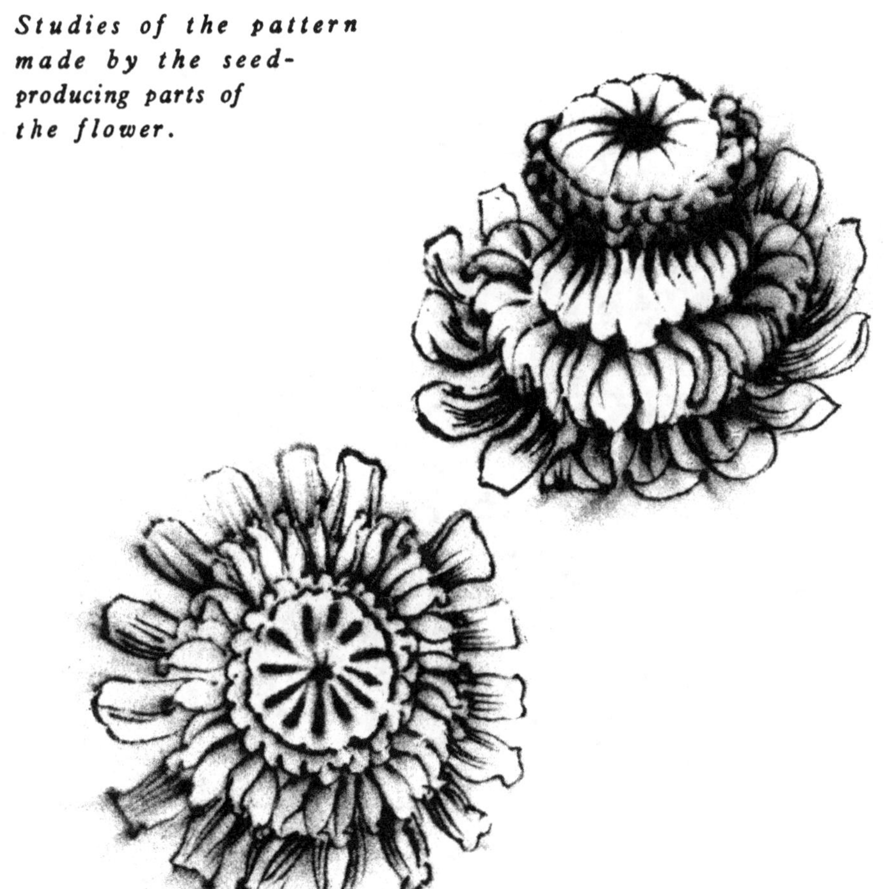

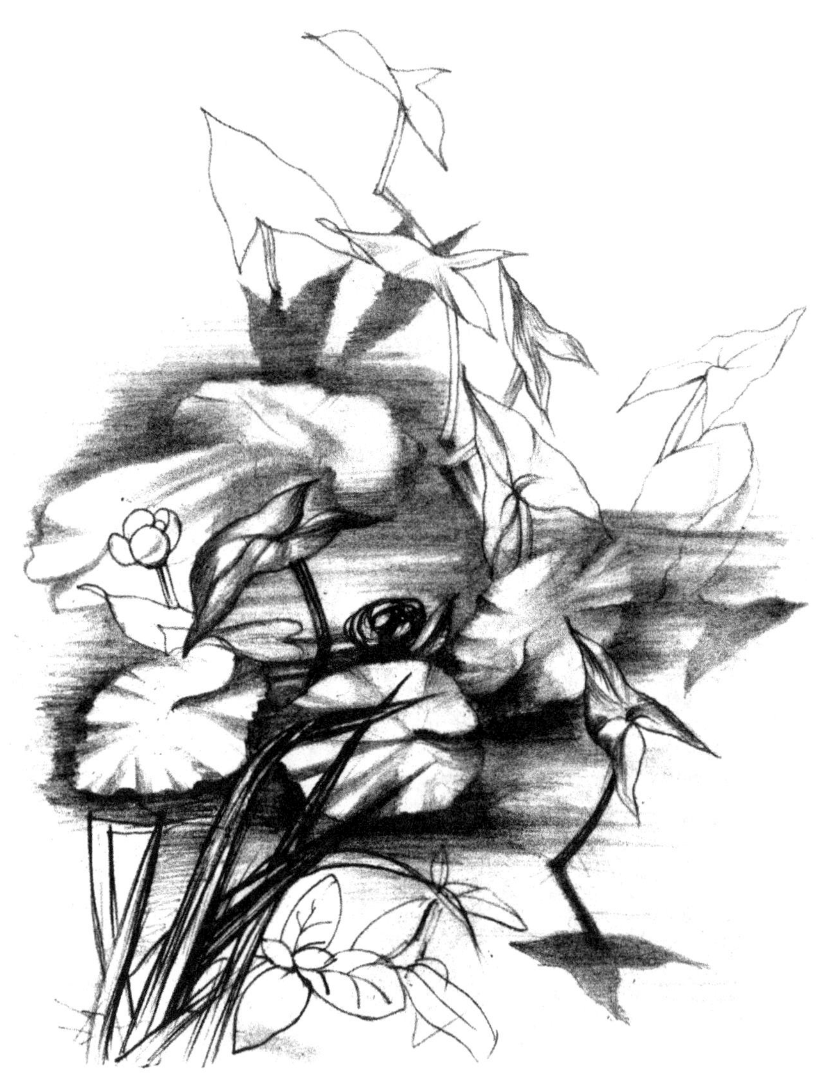

Water-lilies growing in a stream.

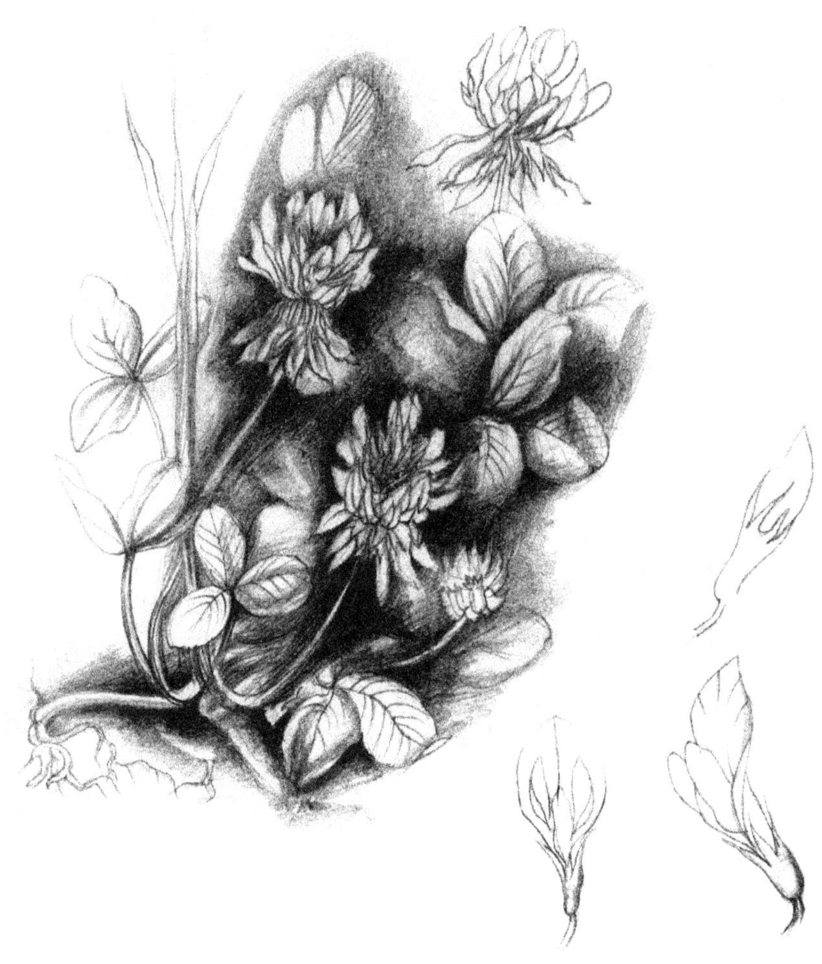

White Clover.

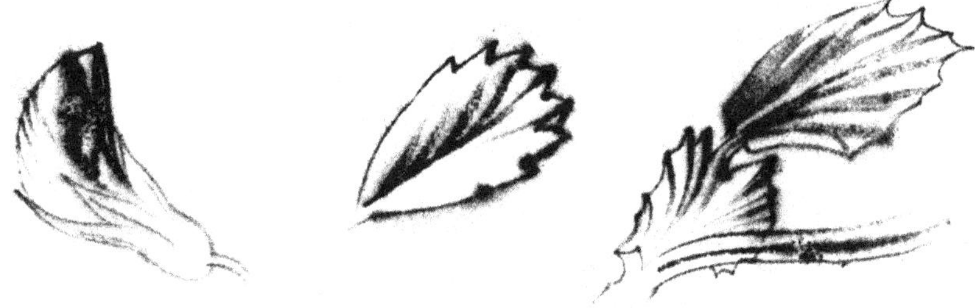

Above and below. Detail brush drawings of Restharrow.

Pencil seemed to be the best medium to use for the clover, which is difficult to draw because the forms are small and delicate. When using a pencil, remember to keep it very sharp. You can use an H. and H.B., and a B. or B.B., on the same drawing, to give variety to the texture. By texture I mean the quality of workmanship that pleases the eye. This is a third important subject for you to learn about and one which is by no means easy. Skilled workmanship, the art of reproducing on paper the satiny, or velvety, or rough look of flowers and leaves, comes only after long practice. You can however begin simply. If you rub charcoal on to rough paper you will see that its texture is quite different from that of a patch of black water-

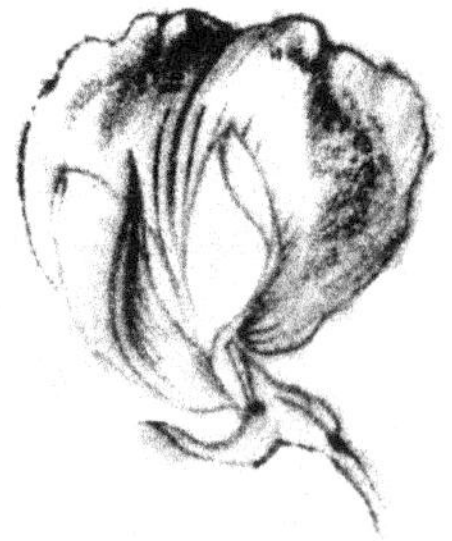

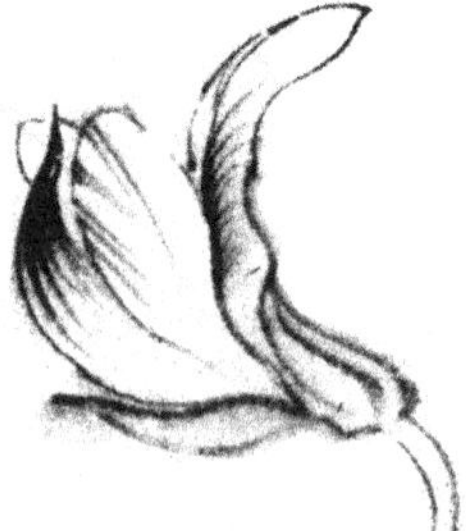

Restharrow.

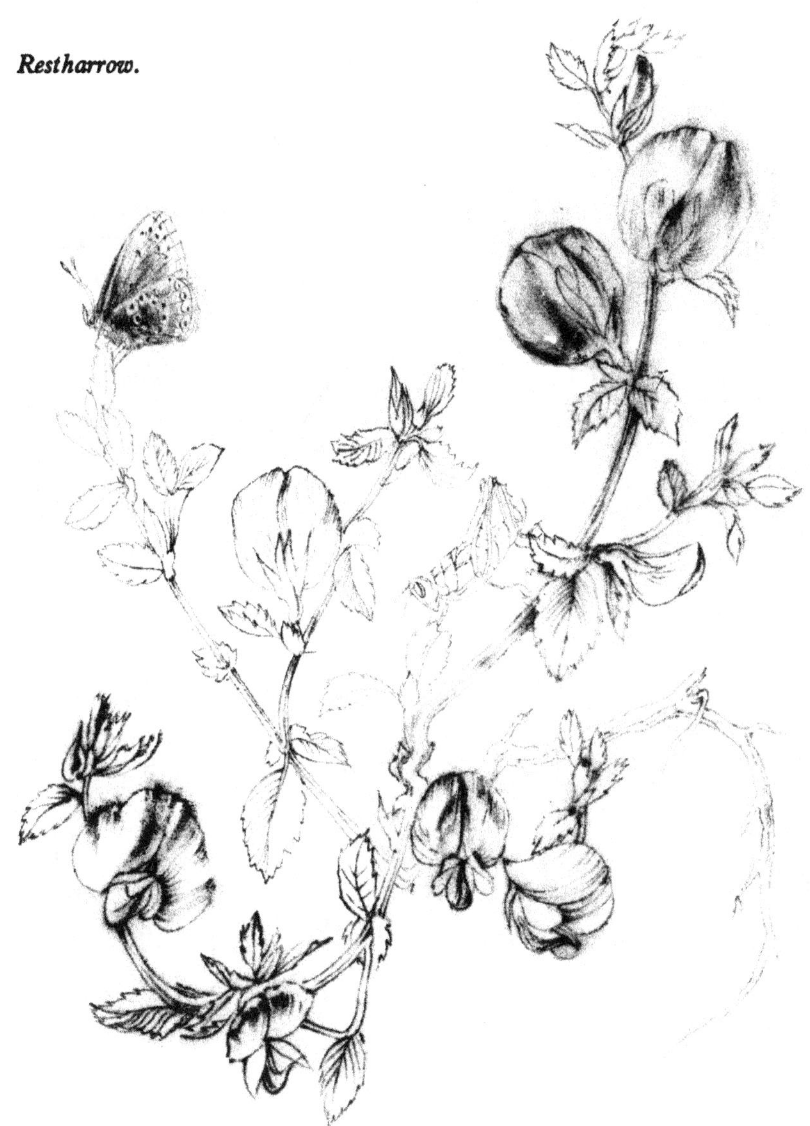

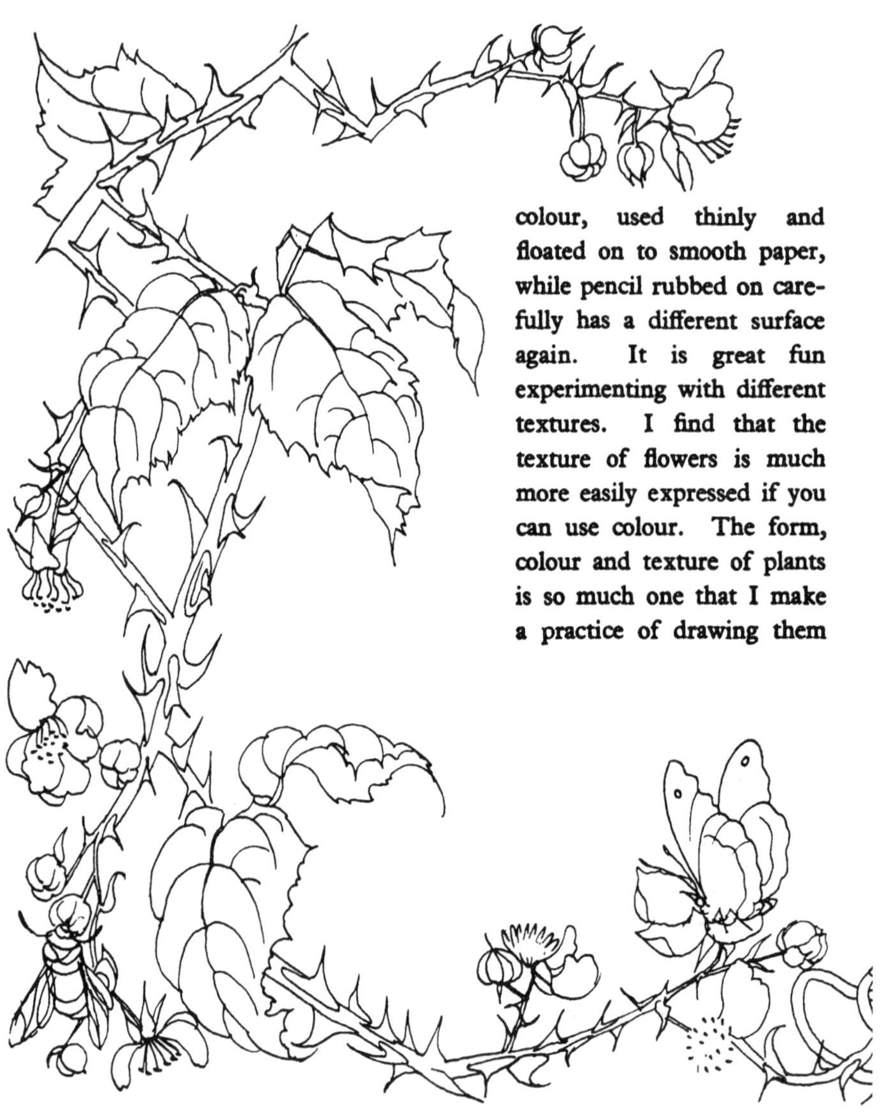

colour, used thinly and floated on to smooth paper, while pencil rubbed on carefully has a different surface again. It is great fun experimenting with different textures. I find that the texture of flowers is much more easily expressed if you can use colour. The form, colour and texture of plants is so much one that I make a practice of drawing them

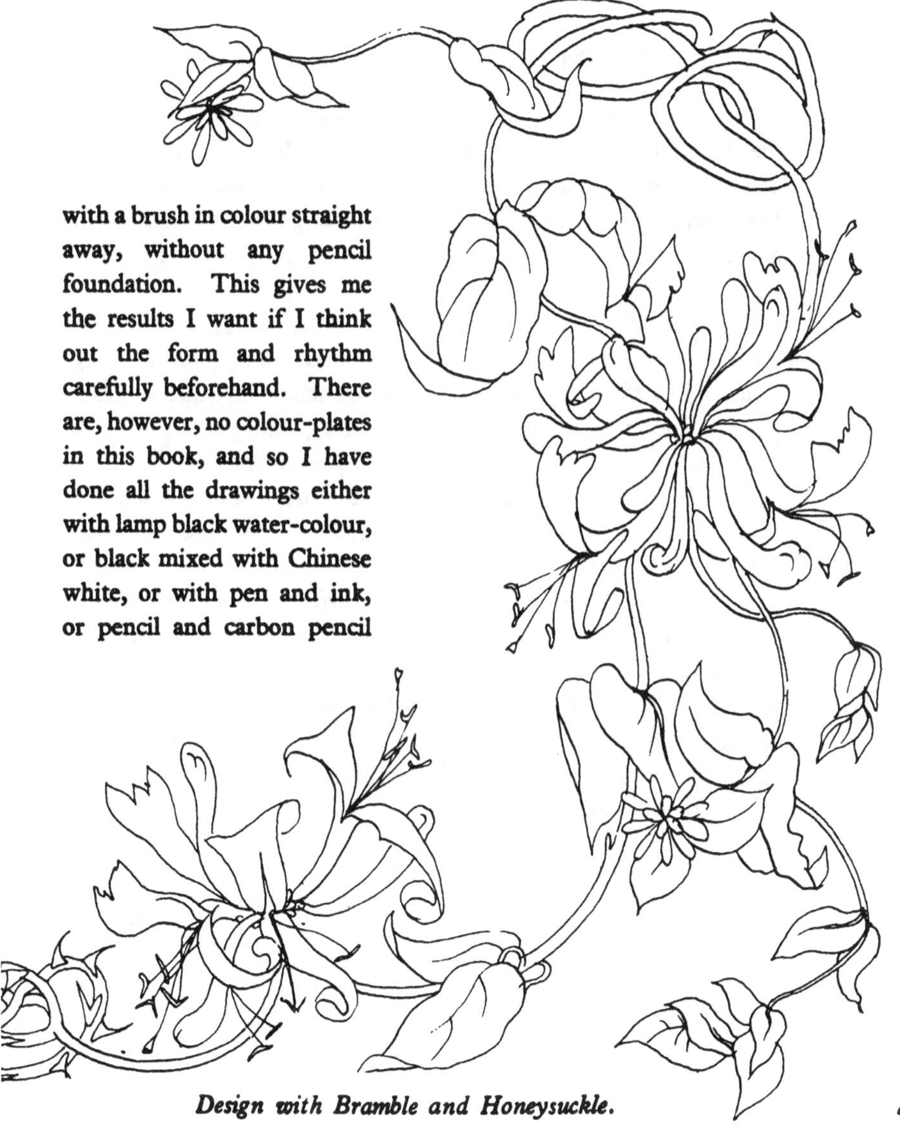

with a brush in colour straight away, without any pencil foundation. This gives me the results I want if I think out the form and rhythm carefully beforehand. There are, however, no colour-plates in this book, and so I have done all the drawings either with lamp black water-colour, or black mixed with Chinese white, or with pen and ink, or pencil and carbon pencil

Design with Bramble and Honeysuckle.

of different richness of tone. I have varied the medium according to the kind of flower represented. Those with particularly silky or delicate texture—rosebay, restharrow, water-lily, snapdragon, goats-beard, are drawn with a brush. I can thus get a clear, clean stroke, and a sweeping line with the tip of the brush, which must have a good point.

Brush-drawing is good practice. You cannot afford to make a mistake. One wavering line or ugly stroke, and your drawing is spoilt. You must practise beforehand on scraps of paper in order to get eye and hand working together nicely, and you must be very quiet and peaceful in your mind while you are painting.

Climbing plants, such as the rose, honeysuckle and bramble, make decorative patterns when twined together, as on pages 40 and 41. Here I have used a plain pen line ; this makes a simple border, in keeping with the printed text. I have had to *formalise* the plants to a certain extent, that is to say, I have used the main shapes and lines only, arranging them to fit into the page, with the curves twining to and fro in a pleasing manner. When the main lines of the design are spaced out, I put in the flowers and leaves, at intervals. This is one way to set about making a decorative design, which can be any shape, to fill any space.

The Foxglove on page 45 is just a portrait of the growing plant, drawn from life in a wood. I picked the bells off another plant first of all to see how they were spaced ; page 44 shows a rough sketch of their alternate arrangement. The bells are rounded, as you see, with light and shade to which you can apply the simple rule I gave you at the beginning of the chapter.

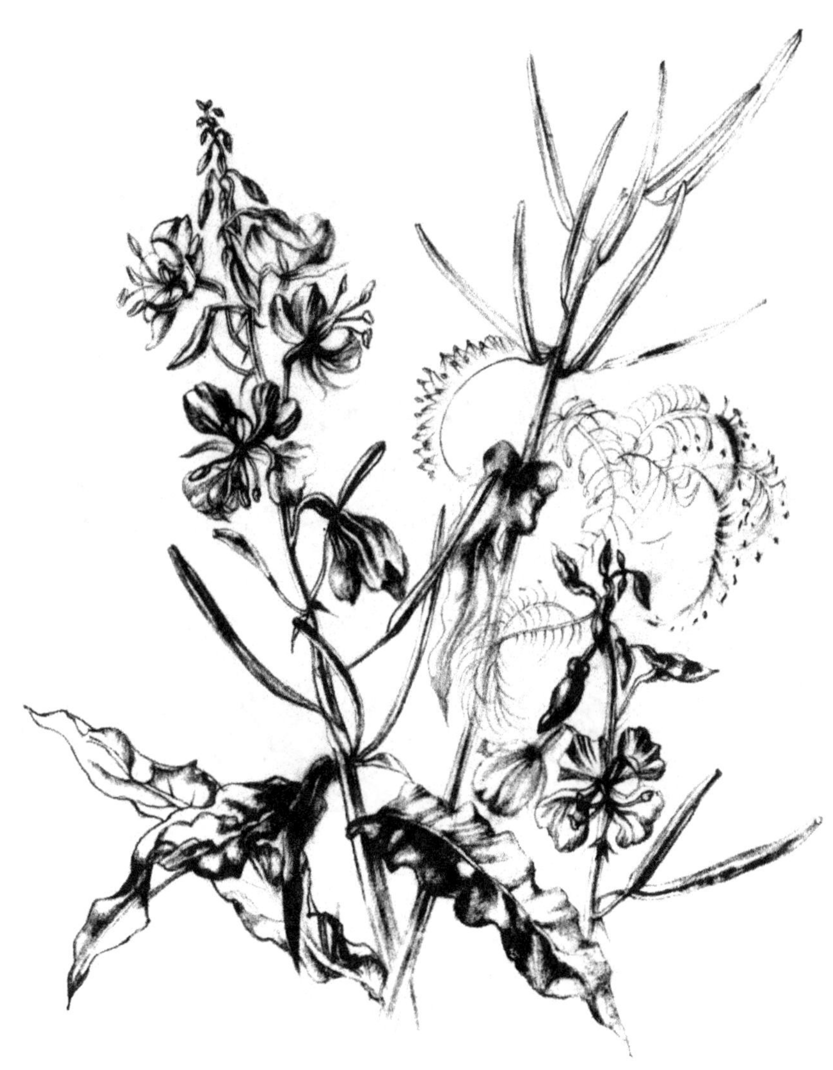

Brush drawing on japanese paper of Rosebay or Fireweed.

Foxgloves.

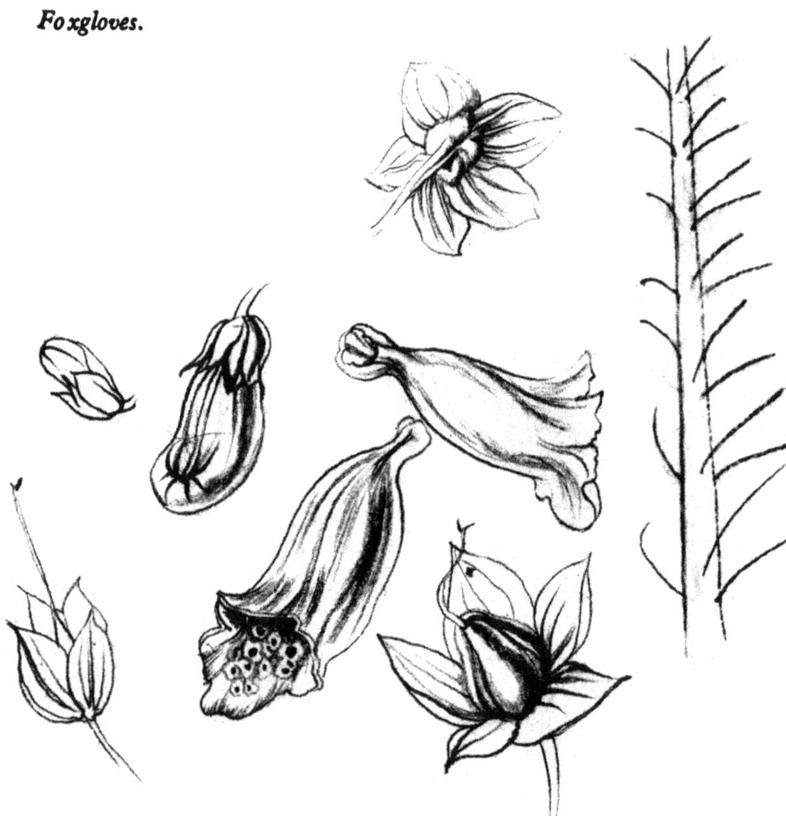

The foxglove is a tall plant ; I have therefore drawn it right down to the bottom of the page. This is a good way of giving an impression of height. The plant thus looks as if it were growing up in front of the page, and you can imagine a distance beyond it.

*** *** ***

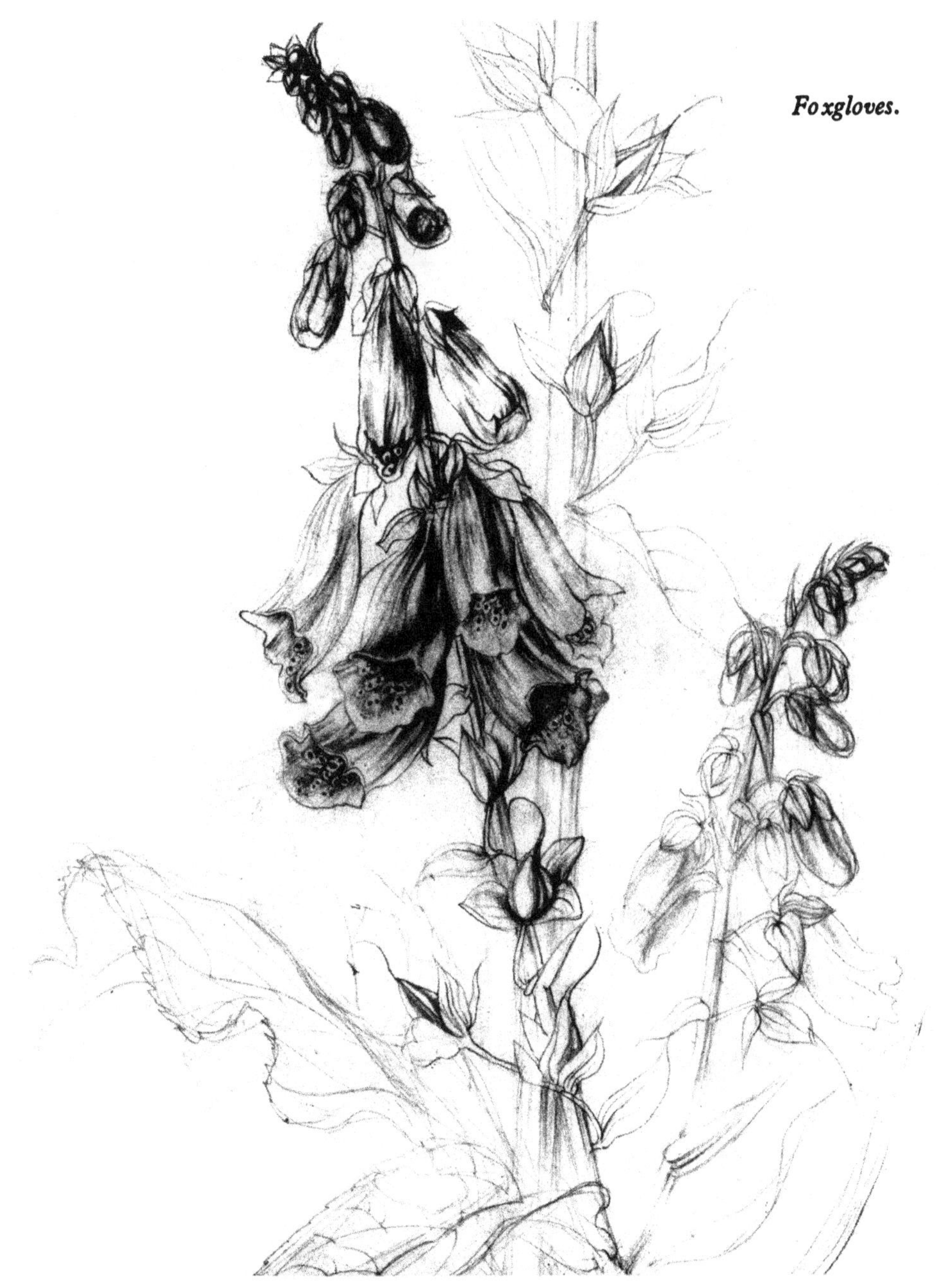

Foxgloves.

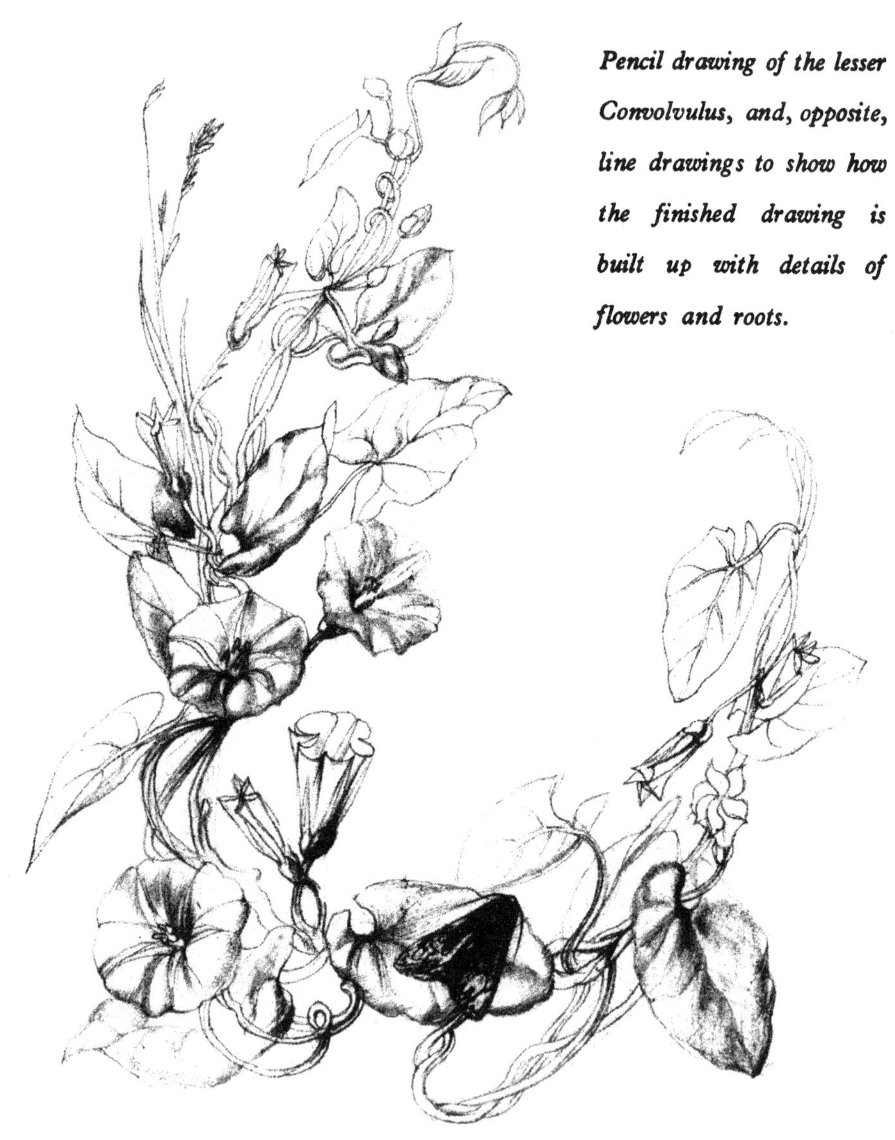

Pencil drawing of the lesser Convolvulus, and, opposite, line drawings to show how the finished drawing is built up with details of flowers and roots.

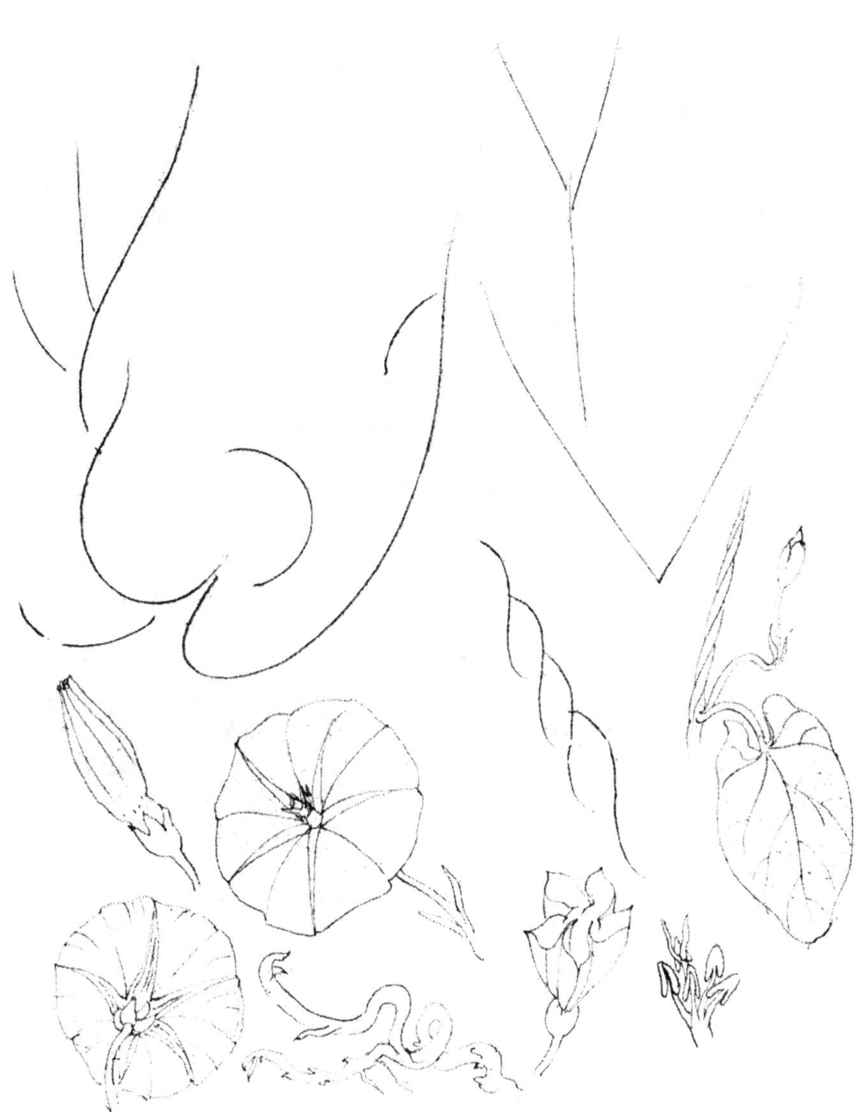

SUMMER FLOWERS

There is no prettier flower than the sweet-scented, pink-and-white lesser convolvulus, or as country folk call it, the bindweed or bellbine ; but it is a dreadful weed. The corkscrew roots twine hither and thither in gardens, here plunging straight down, there twisting near the surface in an underground network most difficult to eradicate ; for the smallest piece spreads in no time, and up comes the bindweed, twining round the garden flowers and eventually smothering them.

Here is a pencil drawing of the flowers and leafy trails (page 46), and opposite, a diagram to show the rhythm of the drawing, and some line sketches of the flower to show its shape. It is formed exactly like a diminutive umbrella. The silky petals stretch between stiff ribs that shut at night, wrapping the petals together like the flaps of the umbrella when closed.

Roots and stems of the bindweed grow alike in a spiral, and so my finished drawing is built up on a wide curve, which is part of the spiral form. But within the main curves is a secondary movement of upright lines. These correspond to the grasses in the finished drawing, and their purpose is to strengthen the shape of the design, which might otherwise appear to be falling to pieces.

When working out compositions of your own in curving shapes, you will probably find that some such upright lines are necessary, and, perhaps, some horizontal lines as well, to steady the whole. Not only are they useful from the point of view of design, but they gave variety—like bass chords sounding in a piece of treble music, or the notes of a violin played in concert with a piano.

*** *** ***

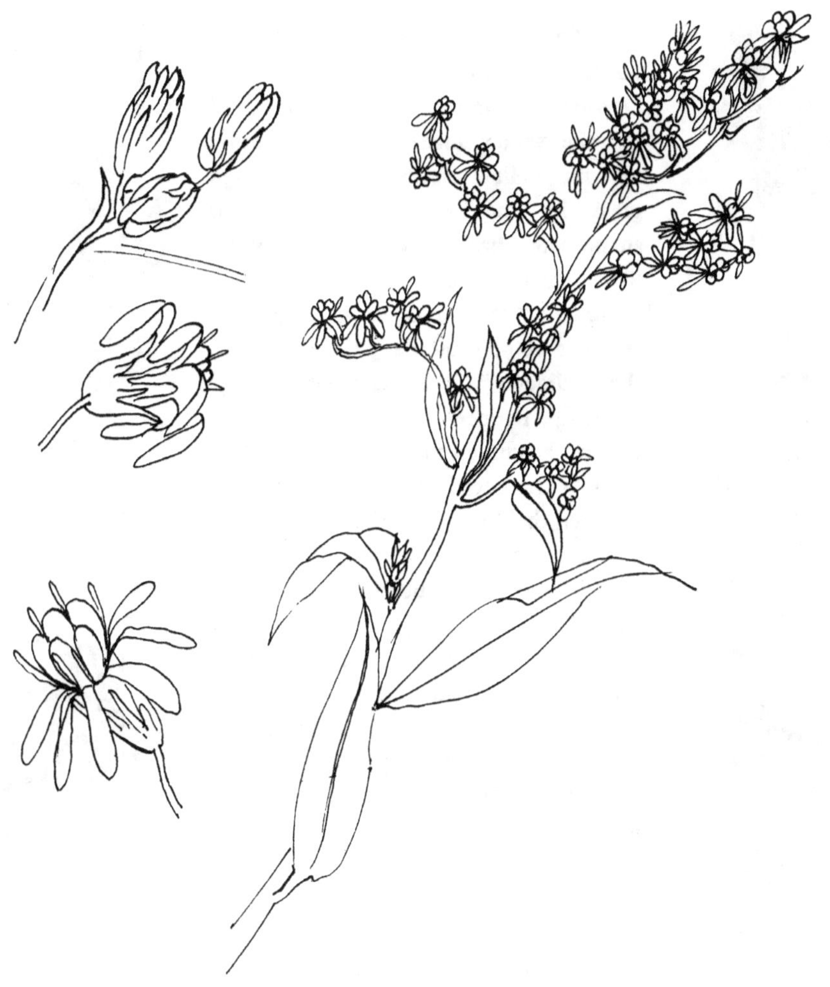

Detail pen-and-ink drawing of Golden Rod.

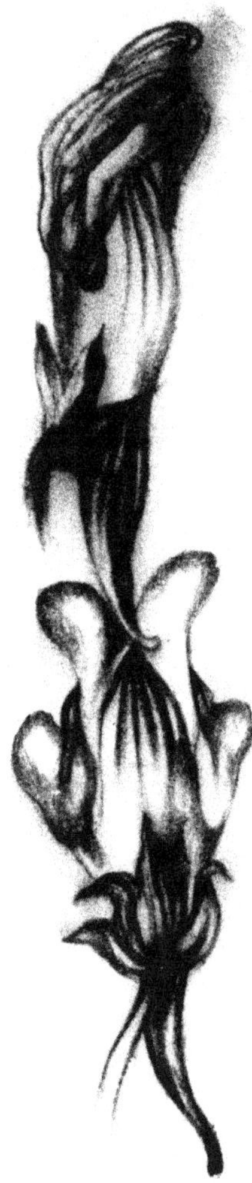

In September, a few late flowers still flourish; Knapweed, Yarrow, Harebells, Deadnettles and, most fascinating of all, the yellow toadflax, which throws up its yellow spikes among rough grass by the wayside. This wild snapdragon has dragon-shaped flowers with fierce faces, most interesting to draw; they look as if they were snarling at one another. If you pinch the "dragon" just below its orange lower-lip, it opens its "jaws" and you can see the curved stamen with its pollen-mass. The bees have to force their way between the "jaws" of the flower which deposits the pollen on their backs and legs, whence it is rubbed off on to other dragon-flowers. Deep down among the green sepals, is the seed-to-be, which grows into pods not unlike closed fists that open when ripe and throw out the seed. In my drawing the pods are formed, but they are not yet ripe and brown.

Brush drawings of the Snapdragon's flowers with "jaws" open and shut, and a half-grown bud.

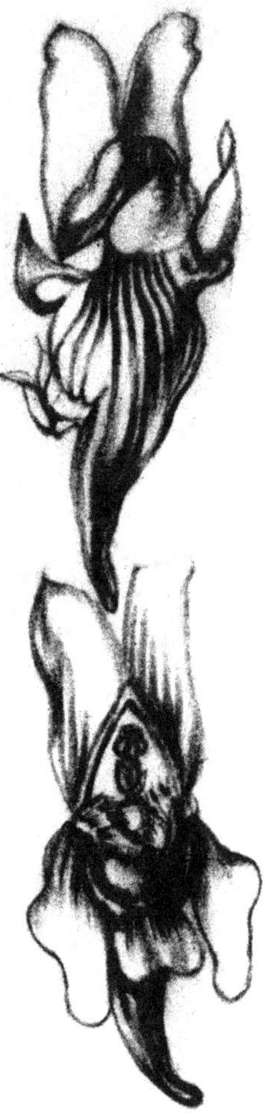

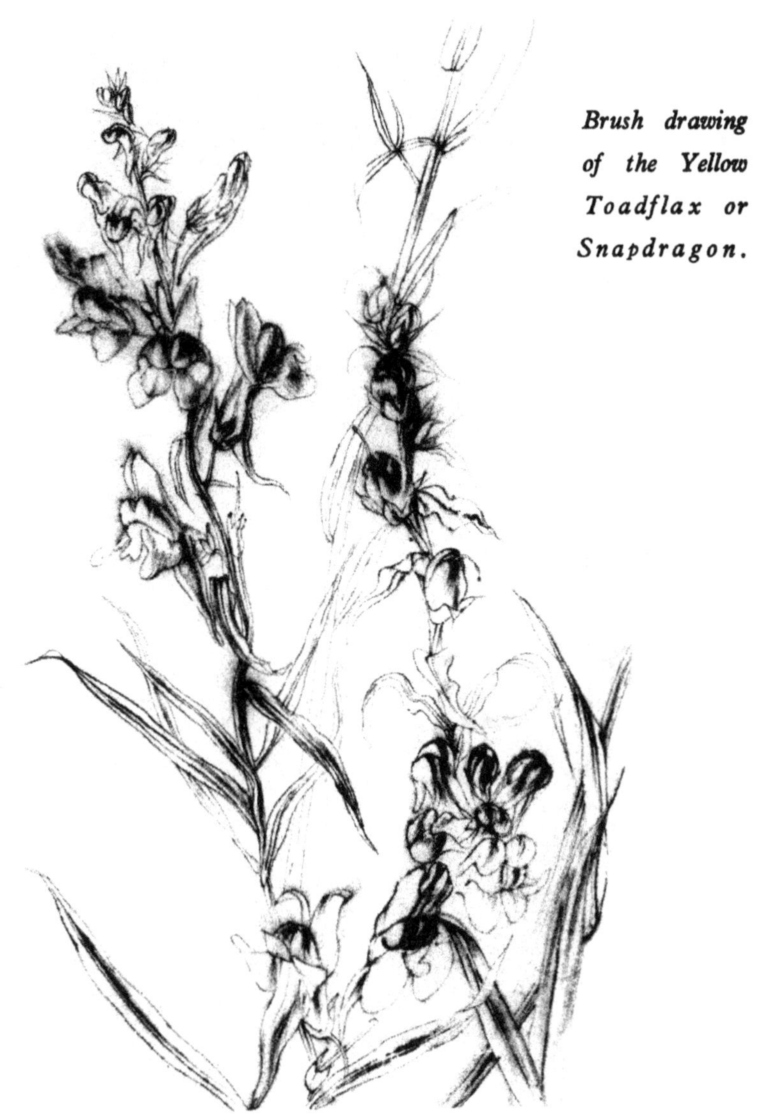

Brush drawing of the Yellow Toadflax or Snapdragon.

AUTUMN BERRIES AND SEEDPODS

Blackberries, pencil drawing.

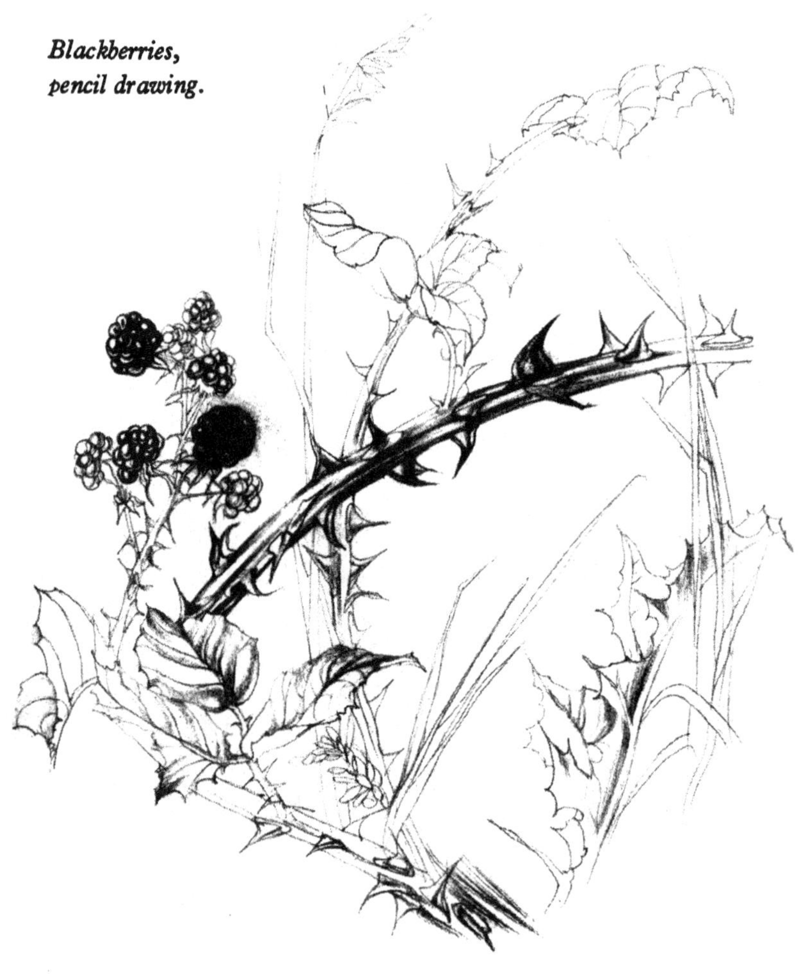

The flowers of some plants produce seeds, whilst others become berries. These, as you know, have a hard stone, or core, within which lies the kernel with its tiny living speck—the future plant—hidden inside. Normally, a seed shed in Autumn germinates in the Spring. But seeds kept in a dry place remain alive for two or more years and will then grow if you plant them. A scientist recently raised a plant from a two-hundred-year-old seed in a museum collection, and wheat found in graves made by the ancient Britons grew when planted. It is said, too, that wheat has germinated when taken from Egyptian tombs many centuries old.

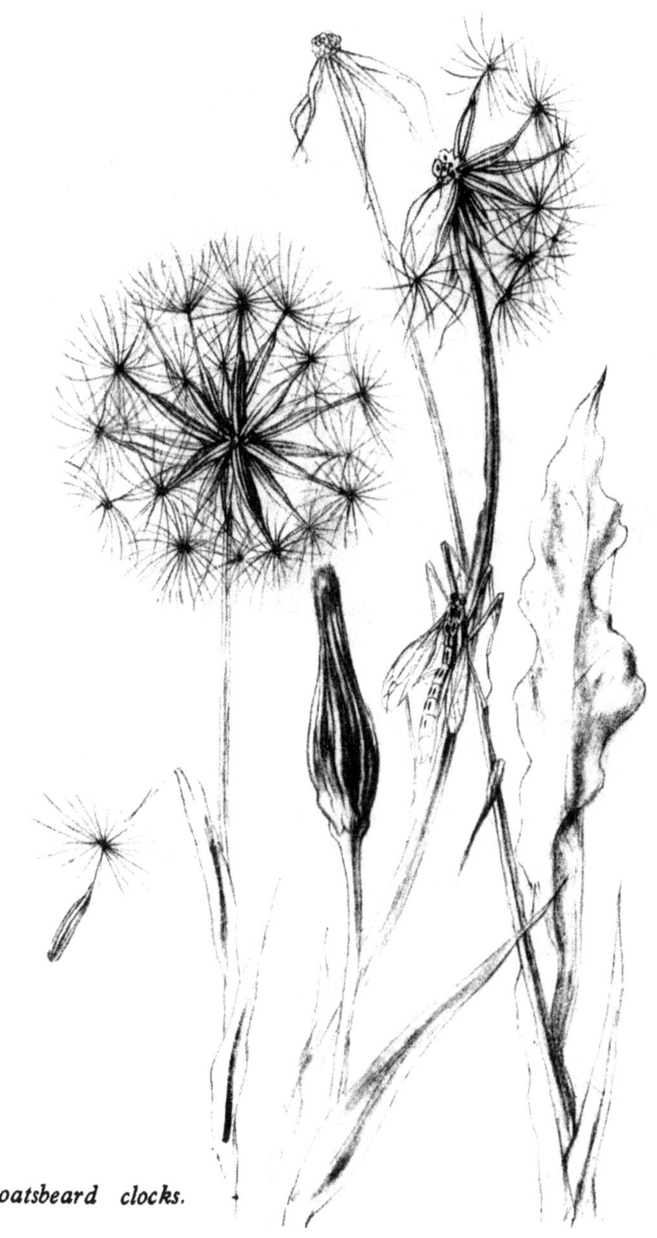

Goatsbeard clocks.

AUTUMN BERRIES AND SEEDPODS

You can collect lovely berries from the autumn hedgerows ; black-berries, red hips of the dog-rose, coral-tinted honeysuckle fruits, and drooping clusters of the poisonous berries of bittersweet. (Page 55). Here and there the broom swings its pods, and the thickets are festooned with hops and tangles of fluffy " Old Man's Beard ". And among the rank grasses, seed-cases of Campion and poppy sway and rustle, scattering abroad their seeds.

These seeds are neatly packed in their cases. In the broom's pods they lie in a row with a paper-like division between each—much as you would arrange eggs in a basket. The case of the poppy has several compartments, each full of seed, and over them an ornamental roof that lifts when the seeds are ripe, showing a row of apertures, like windows, through which the seeds pour out. The urn of the campion is closed at first and opens when the seeds ripen. These seed-urns have fat, satisfying shapes ; I think you will enjoy drawing them.

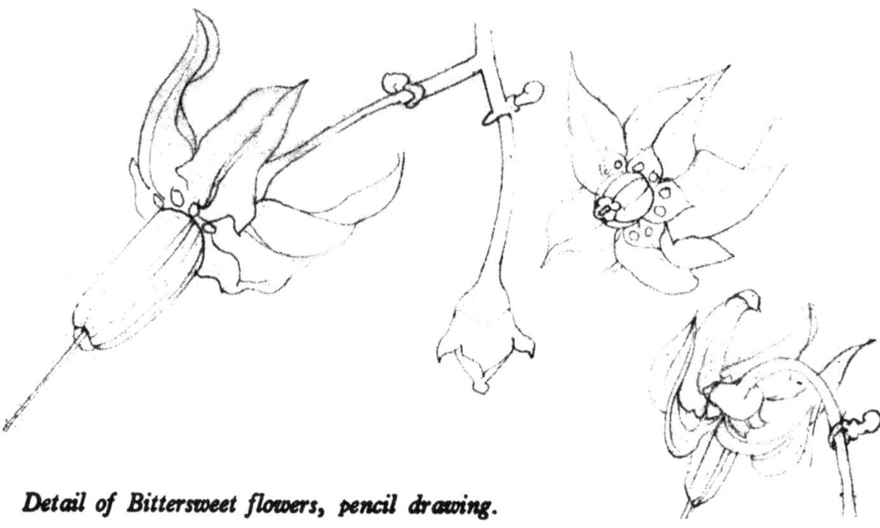

Detail of Bittersweet flowers, pencil drawing.

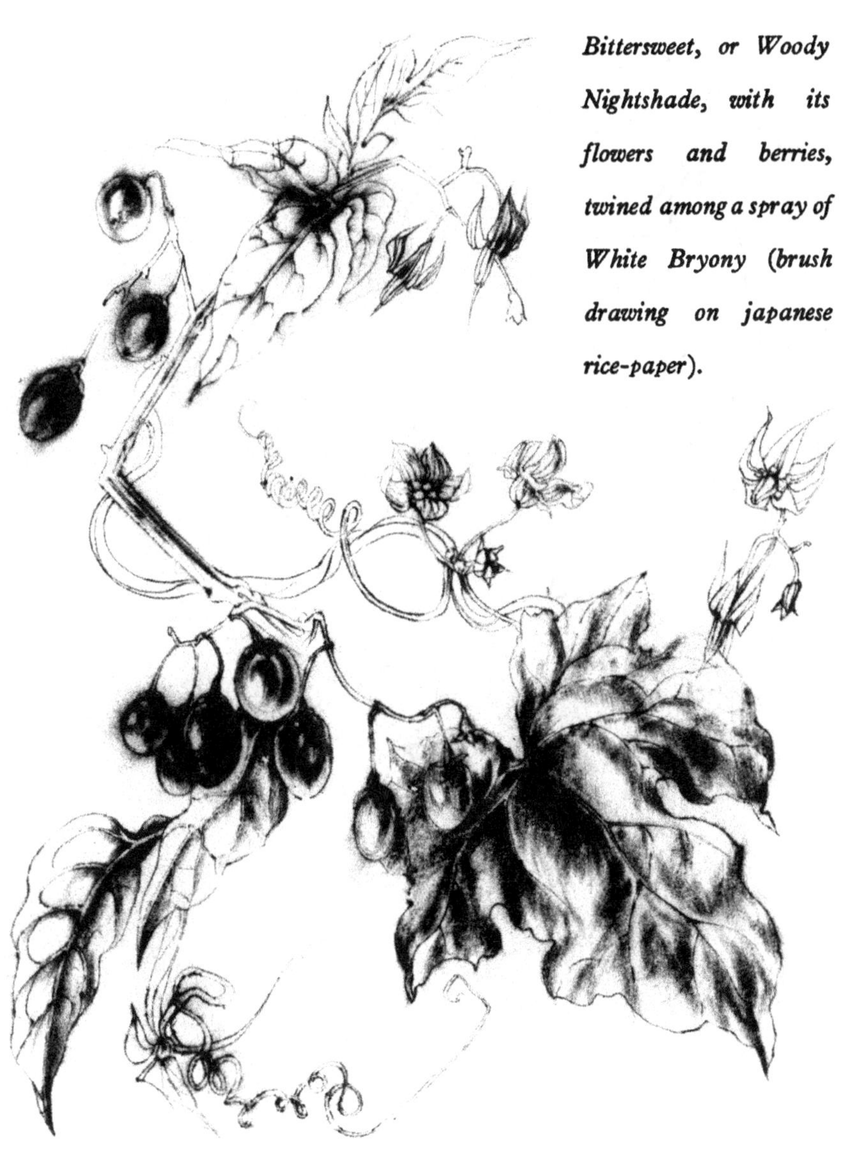

Bittersweet, or Woody Nightshade, with its flowers and berries, twined among a spray of White Bryony (brush drawing on japanese rice-paper).

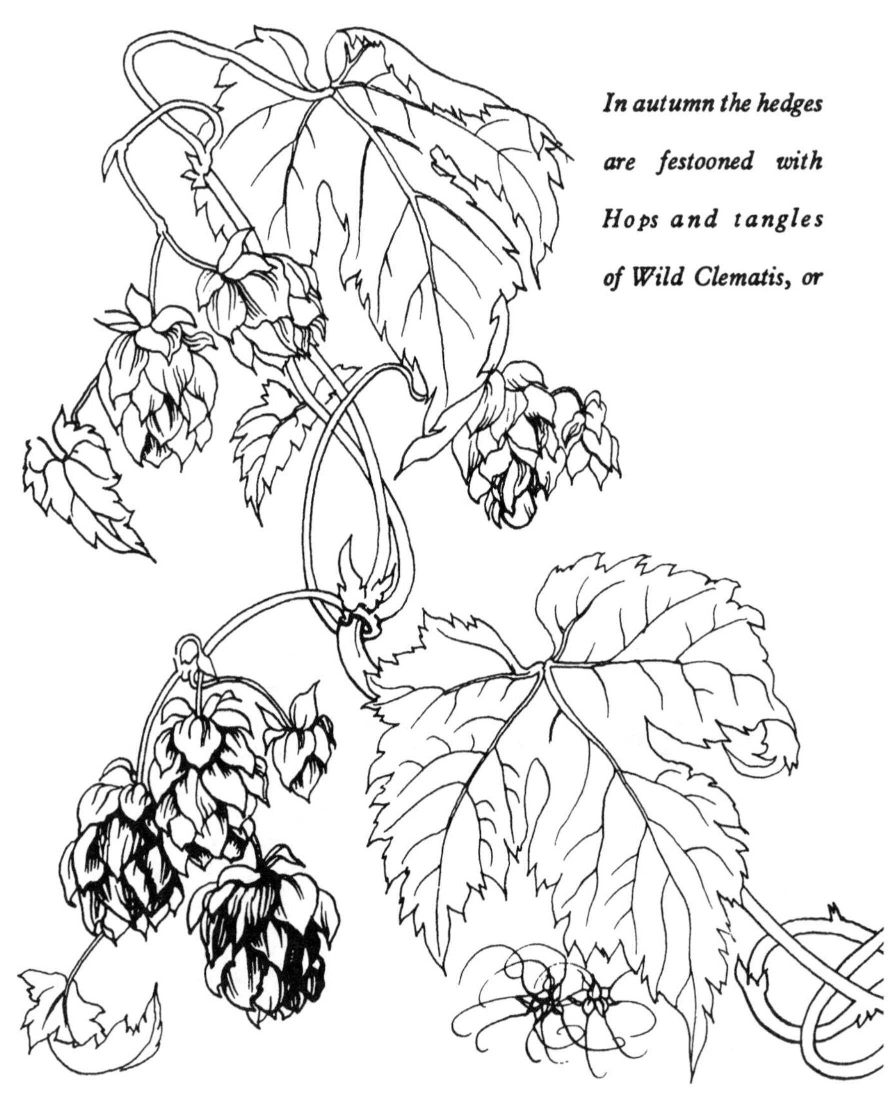

In autumn the hedges are festooned with Hops and tangles of Wild Clematis, or

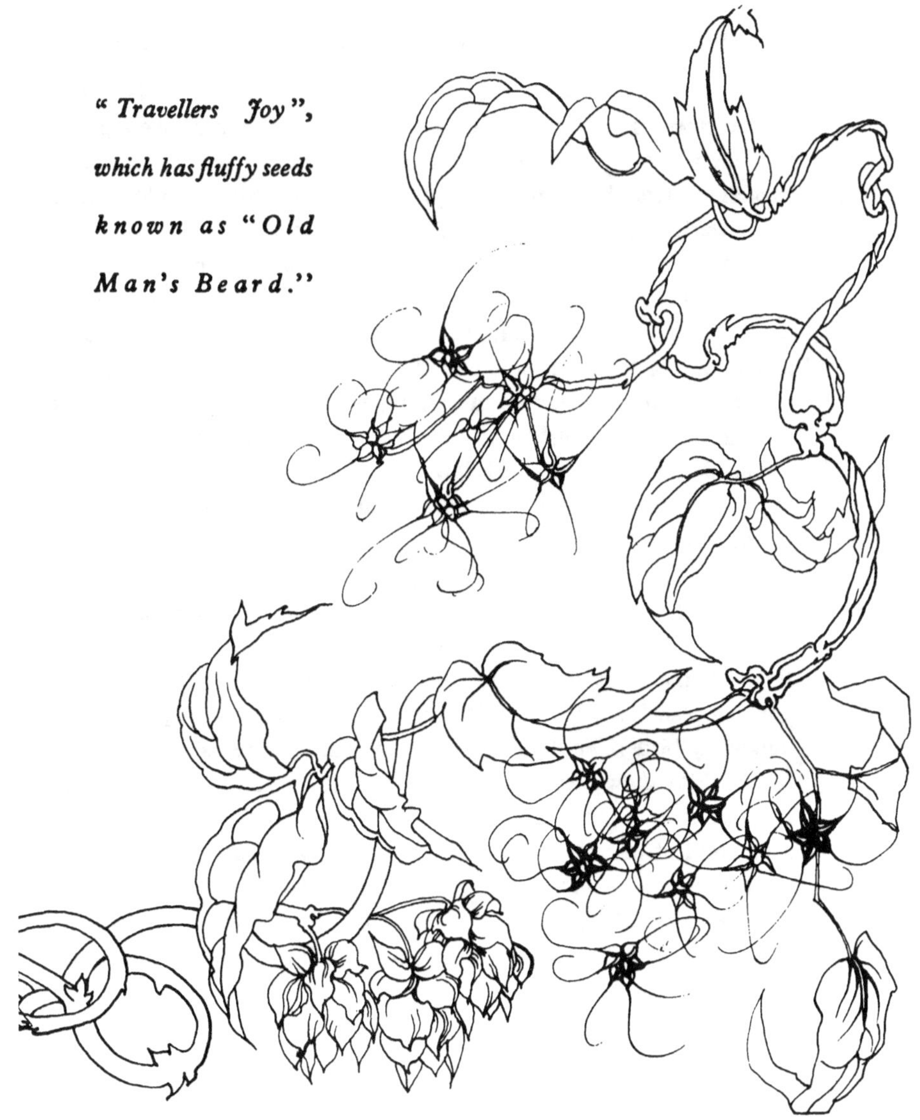

"Travellers Joy", which has fluffy seeds known as "Old Man's Beard."

AUTUMN BERRIES AND SEEDPODS

Here are some characteristic forms (pages 60 and 61). The scales on the ripening knapweedhead (page 61, figs. 1, 2 and 3) overlap like tiles on a roof, or feathers on a bird's back. Their arrangement suggested to me three patterns (figs. 4, 5 and 6). No. 5 would make a needlework design—a border perhaps, for a tapestry. Nos. 4 and 6 could be simply carried out with the wavy criss-cross lines drawn in green chalk and the straight ones in grey or black. Arranged to cover a large sheet of paper, this would make a pleasing design for a folder, or portfolio, in which to keep all your flower-drawings. A collection of these would be interesting as a record of the flowers that grow in your neighbourhood. It will be much more worth doing than a collection of dreary pressed flowers. These have neither colour nor form when dried, and are as unlike growing plants as a mummy is unlike a living person.

When you travel to a new neighbourhood you can add to your collection by drawing the flowers that grow there. Each soil has, of course, its characteristic plants, which vary from place to place. In England, the chalk downs, for instance, are covered with tiny close-growing plants, a coloured carpet of thyme and restharrow, eyebright, milkwort, birds-foot, lotus and companula. There is not space in this book to show them to you, so I must leave you to discover them for yourselves. Different flowers grow in the woods among sand and loam and leaf-mould ; foxgloves and bluebells and spurge, anemones, primroses, yellow pimpernel and tormentil, and that strange, ghostly plant, enchanter's nightshade. You must go to boggy lands (in the New Forest and Devonshire in England) for bog asphodel, buckbean,

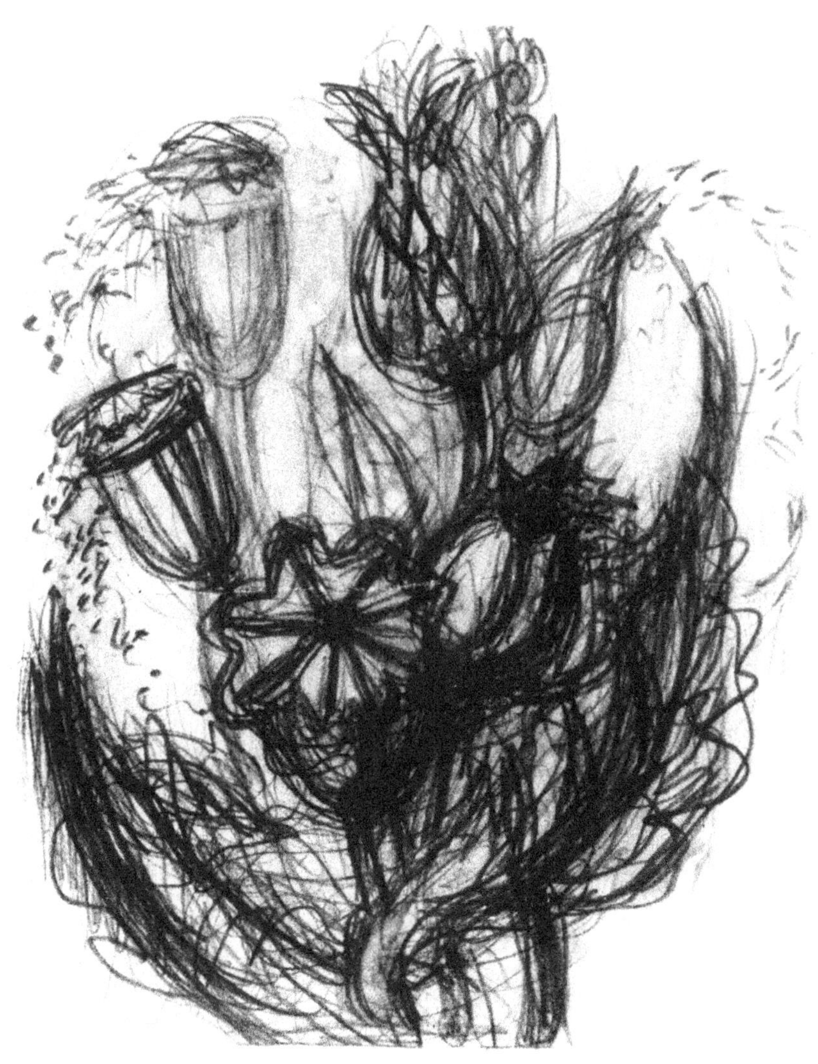

Rough pencil sketch for the chalk drawing of seed-pods overleaf.

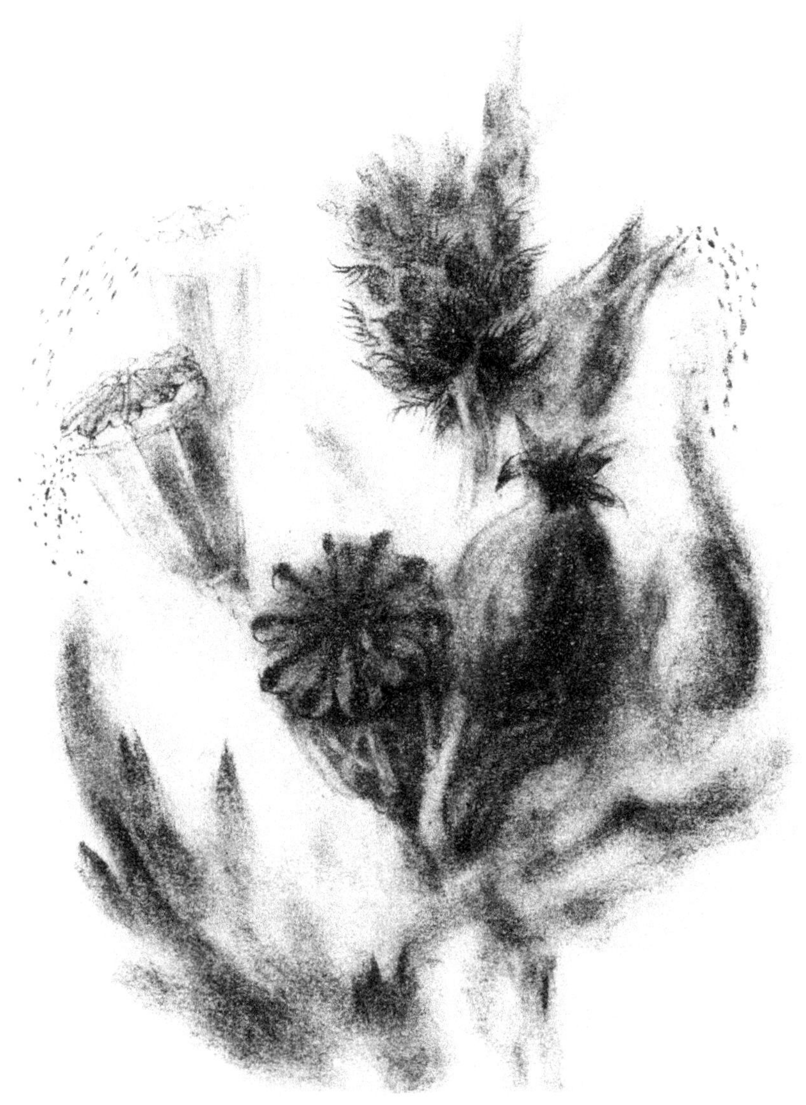

Chalk drawing of seed-pods, Poppy left and centre, Campion right, and Knapweed above.

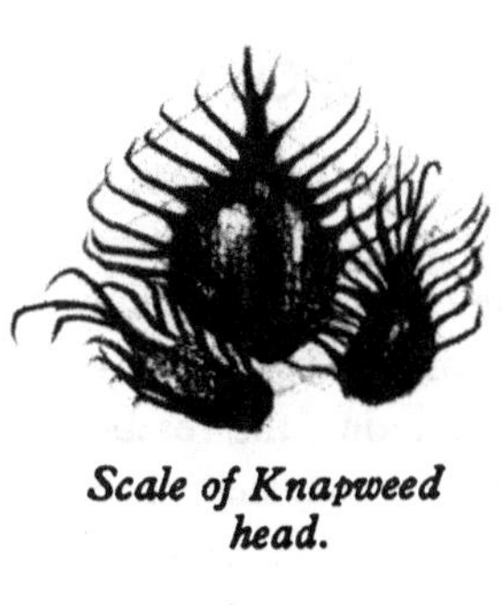

Scale of Knapweed head.

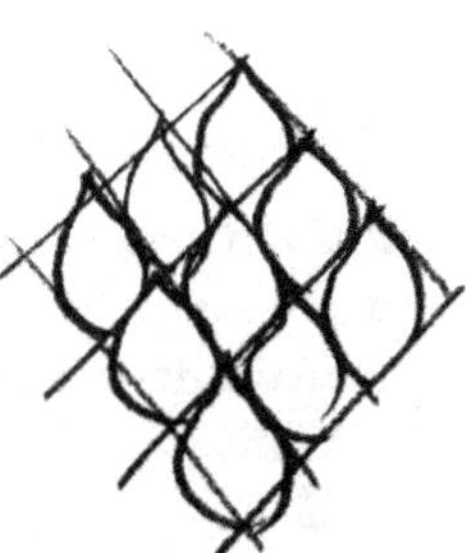

Showing regular arrangement of scales.

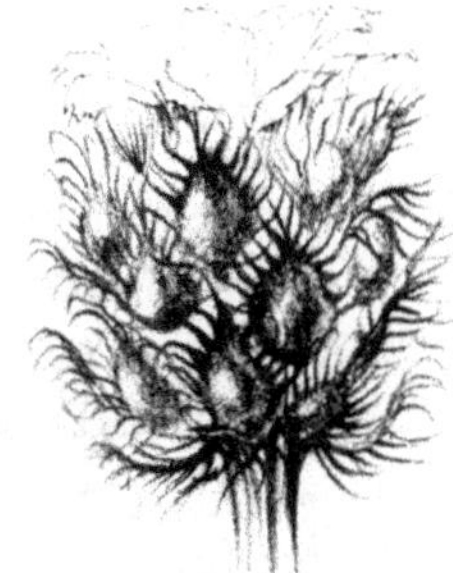

Knapweed head.

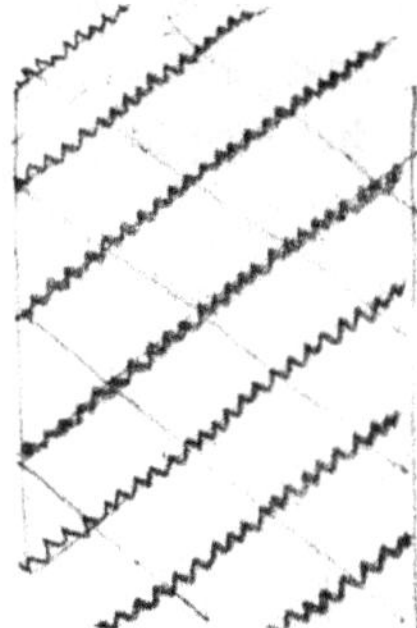

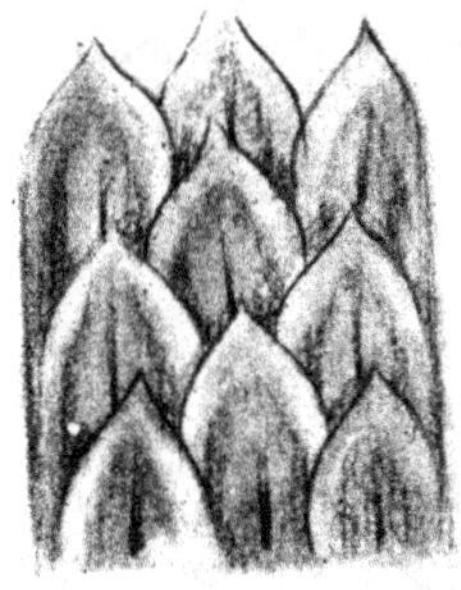

Simple designs suggested by criss-cross arrangement of scales.

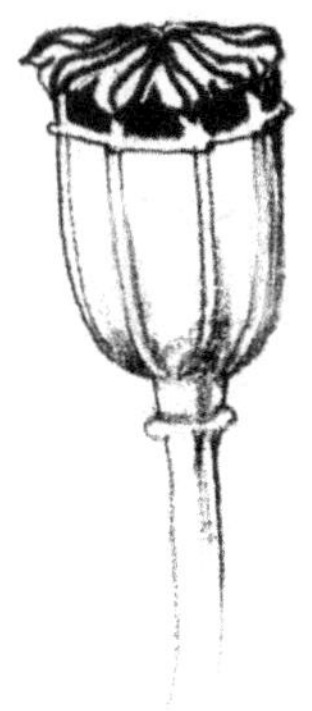

Poppy seed-pods.

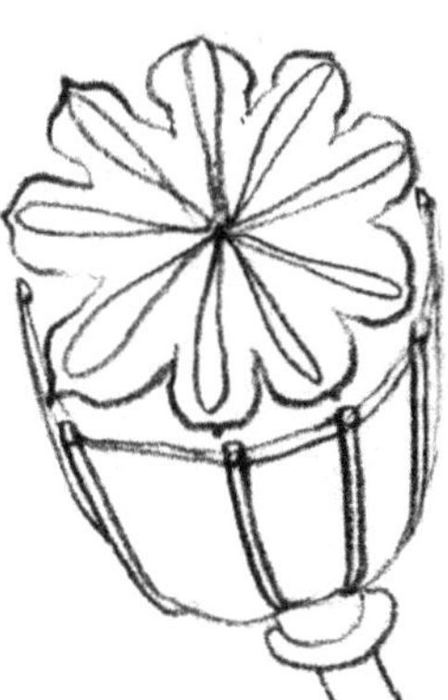

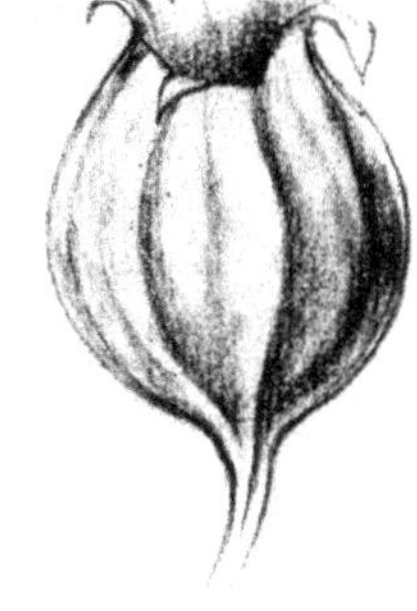

Seed-case of the White Campion.

and sundew, and to the heaths and moorlands for heather and harebells. If you live in America, you will find an even greater variety to choose from, for the flowers on the Atlantic side of the continent are totally different from those on the Pacific coast. A few of the flowers I have shown you grow wild both in England and in America, the rosebay for one (in America it is known as fireweed), and the woody nightshade or bittersweet, and the knapweed; while the golden rod, of which I have given a detail sketch, is a garden flower in England but grows wild in America, where it is the national flower of Maryland.

And now I will leave you to make your flower drawings in your own way; and I wish you joy in the making of them.

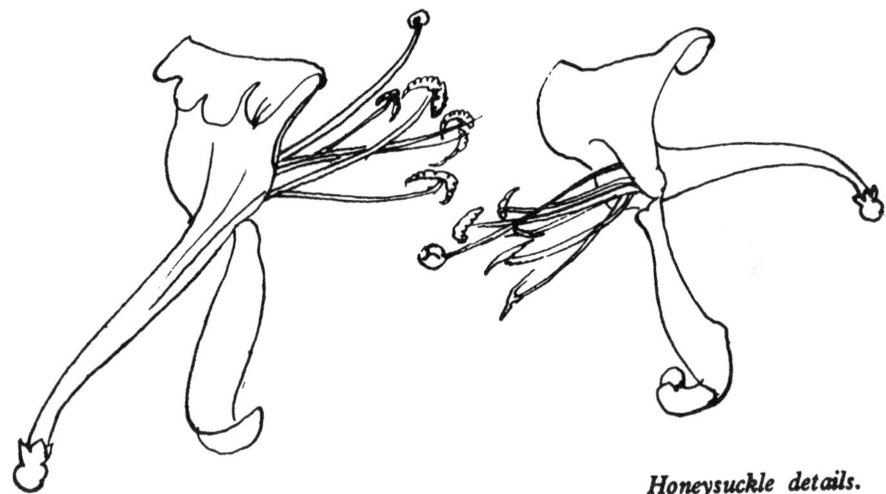

Honeysuckle details.

"Lords and Ladies" and Deadnettle.

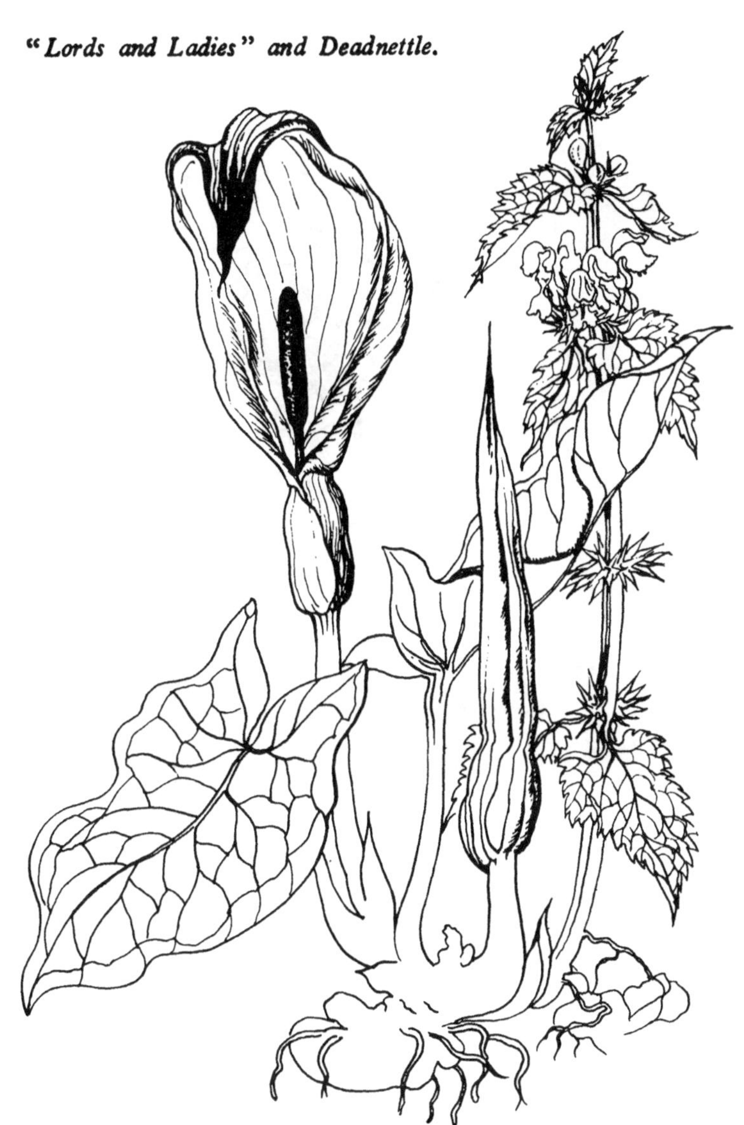

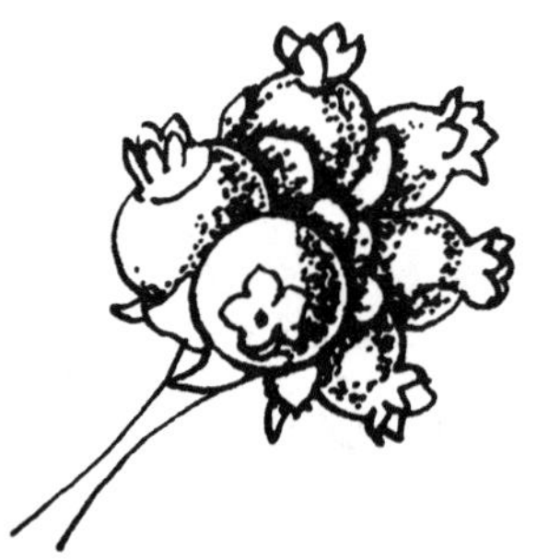

Coachwhip Publications

CoachwhipBooks.com

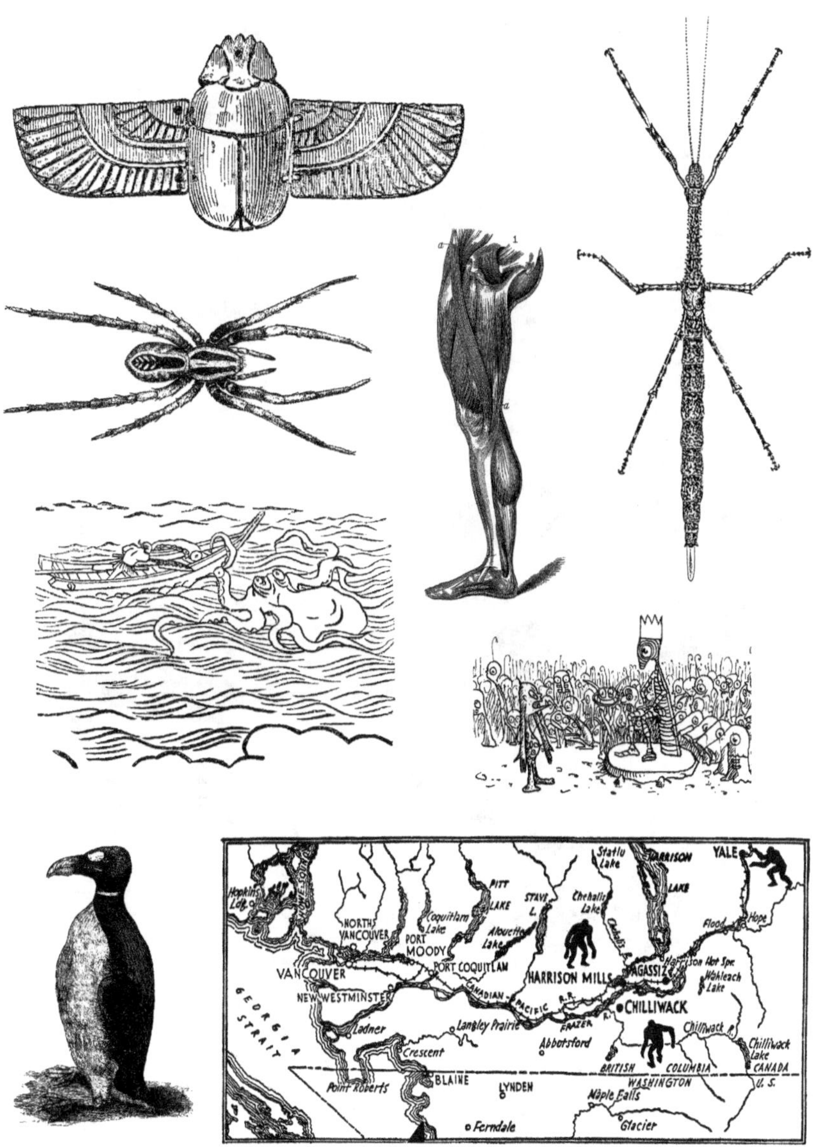

Coachwhip Publications
CoachwhipBooks.com

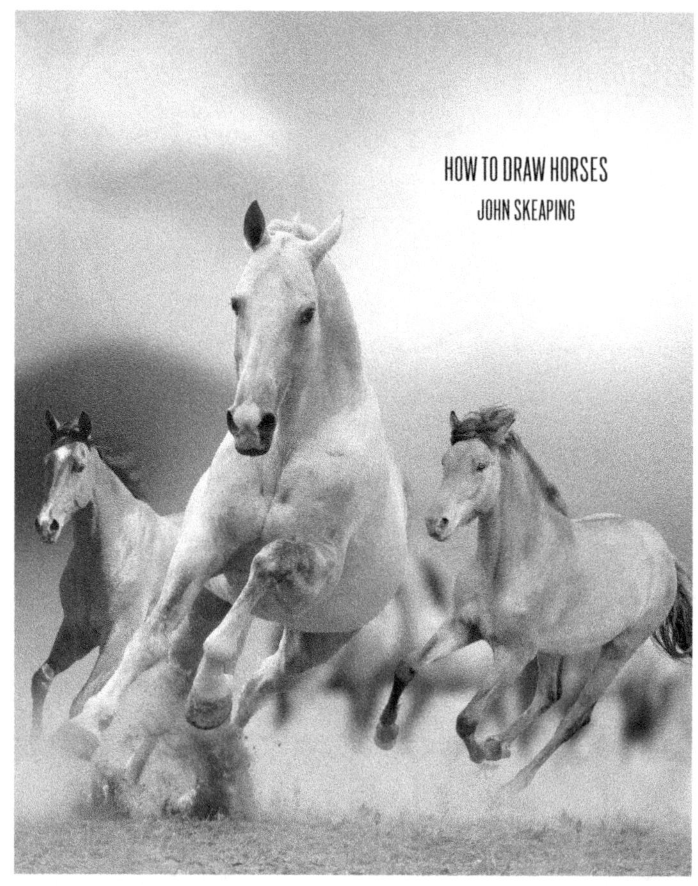

ISBN 978-1-61646-190-4

COACHWHIP PUBLICATIONS
COACHWHIPBOOKS.COM

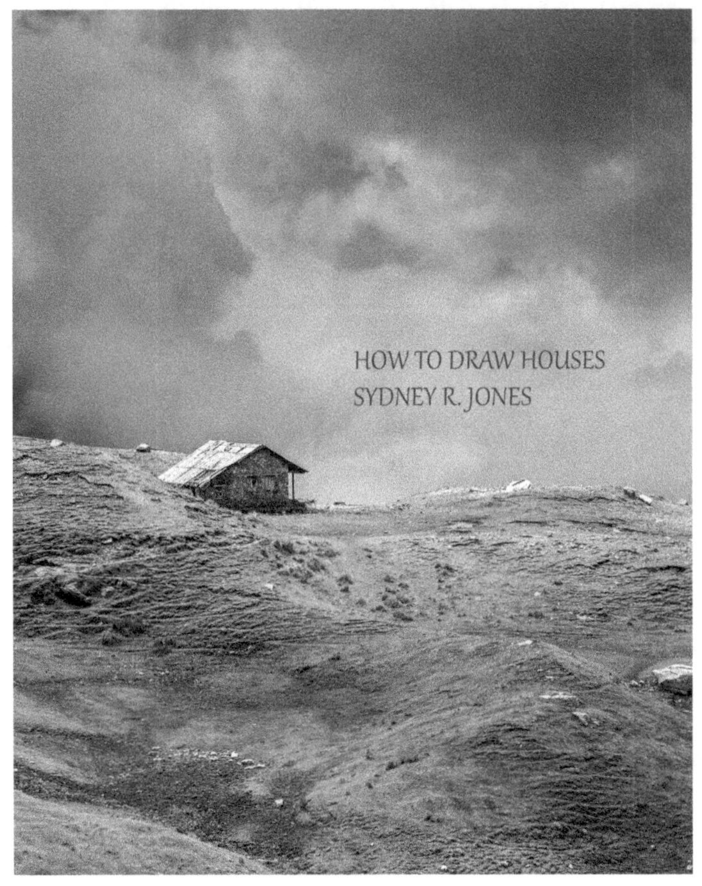

ISBN 978-1-61646-195-9

www.ingramcontent.com/pod-product-compliance
Lightning Source LLC
LaVergne TN
LVHW081301100826
845148LV00005B/942

* 9 7 8 1 6 1 6 4 6 1 9 6 6 *